WILL YOU TRADE

YOUR DREAMS

for HIS?

WILL YOU TRADE
YOUR DREAMS

for HIS?

BETH EASTMAN

Outskirts Press, Inc.
Denver, Colorado

Outskirts Press, Inc.
http://www.outskirtspress.com

ISBN: 978-1-4327-5551-5

Outskirts Press and the "OP" logo are trademarks belonging to Outskirts Press, Inc.

PRINTED IN THE UNITED STATES OF AMERICA

This book is dedicated to my daughter who was truly a gift from above.

Meredith Elisabeth
February 16, 2007- April 14, 2008

"Lo, children are a heritage of the Lord; and the fruit of the womb is His reward." (Psalm 127:3, KJV).

Table of Contents

Introduction: Shattered Dreams 1

1 Flattened 3
2 Raging Rivers 11
3 War.. 19
4 The Blessings of Birth 29
5 Held 35
6 Return to Me 45
7 Miracle Meredith 51
8 Home.. 67
9 Savor Every Moment 73
10 Surrender... 79
11 Finality... 83
12 God Whispered "Fourteen" 89
13 Meredith the Missionary 93
14 Trading Dreams.. 99

Acknowledgments.. 107
References 113

Introduction:
Shattered Dreams

Growing up, I always wanted to be a wife and mother. I fulfilled those lifelong dreams when I married Hunt on Aug. 21, 2004, and gave birth to our daughter 2 1/2 years later. As I held Meredith for the first time, I felt that I hadn't really lived until that moment. I remember holding her skin to skin in the hospital just savoring that feeling. I knew she would be my best friend and that I would never love like that again. But in January 2008 all my dreams collapsed. Early in the month, six months pregnant with my second child, a son, I went into labor prematurely. At the same time, the marital abuse I'd been hiding from friends and families was exposed and Meredith, just 11 months old, was diagnosed with brain cancer on January 24, 2008. I was laid bare.

These events tested my strength, my endurance and my acceptance of God's plan for the lives of my children and myself. Each one by itself was devastating. But combined, they stripped away all of my pretenses and left me exposed for everyone to see and judge. I was deeply disappointed by God, by the man I committed to "love and cherish till death do us part" and, most all, by my own self. For 31 years, I had escaped personal tragedy; suddenly it was all I could see and I couldn't hide from it. I was forced to my knees. But I am thankful to have fallen at the feet of my Lord, Jesus Christ.

I always knew that God made me to be a wife and mother. It was my desire as soon as I was old enough to comprehend its joys. Through Meredith's life and illness, Tyler's birth and a shattered marriage, God has revealed a much bigger purpose for me. My children saved my life. With each "crisis" came freedom and with that freedom came purpose. In the midst of complete devastation and pain, God's mercies were revealed and I had to trade my dreams of being a mother and wife for the person God truly created me to be.

My Prayer: Be merciful to me, O Lord, as I share the story You gave me. Although my eyes grow weak with sorrow, my soul and my body with grief, I know that you will give me the strength I need to share with others what my circumstances taught me. Use my anguish and weakness to glorify You and to show others walking through painful situations that without You there is no victory and no peace. Thank you Lord for being the writer of my story. I pray it blesses all who come in contact with it. (Psalms 31:9-10).

1

Flattened

Carepage Entry: Saturday, Jan. 26, 2008 10:15am

Dear Friends and Family,

Thank you so much to all of you who have been flexible with our family in the last few weeks. I have no idea who knows what, so here is an update on our past and current situation.

Two weeks ago, Hunt got very sick with the stomach flu, Monday through Thursday. Meredith then got what we thought was the stomach flu the following Monday and Tuesday. I got the flu Wednesday and went into preterm labor that night. Hunt and I went to WakeMed Thursday morning and I was admitted and stayed until Tuesday of the following week. Meredith got the flu (again, we thought it was the flu) Friday, so the day I was discharged (Tuesday) my mother and I went back to the emergency room to get Meredith treated. She was in the ER till 3 a.m. and then we were sent home. *She continued to throw up for the next two days. We spent Thursday and half of Friday in the Children's Emergency Room.*

Yesterday, as the flu treatments continued and we were waiting to be seen, my child was not getting better. I completely flipped out and demanded the doctors come see her. At that point, her eyes were rolling back in her head and she seemed unresponsive. I knew (mother's instinct) that I could not sit there and let the "flu" run its course anymore. Meredith ended up seizing and her sodium levels dropped dramatically. We were admitted to the Pediatric Intensive Care Unit (PICU) for a CT scan and found out that Meredith has not had the flu. Meredith has a brain tumor in the fourth ventricle of her brain. I will spare you the details of the rest of the day. Let's just say, we are all in shock.

We are now at Duke in the PICU, one of the best. She will have an MRI today and surgery Monday to remove the tumor. We will know more tomorrow morning when we discuss the MRI with the pediatric neurosurgeon. We need a ton of prayer—pray the tumor is benign, easy to remove and no chemotherapy will be needed. Pray for her brain stem to not be affected. Pray for our families as they try to support and get through this with us. Just pray, pray, pray. I will eventually need help in other areas, but right now we need you to start the prayer chains and ask the Lord for a miracle.

As far as the baby in the oven, Tyler, he is no longer trying to get out, thank you Lord. I am supposed to be on bed rest for two weeks but, as you can imagine, my bed rest has yet to start. I am trying to stay horizontal as much as possible. I know some of you have called our home and my cell and have probably thought we dropped off the face of this Earth. We are still here—just not at home—and we don't know when we will be home again.

When you're a mother, you will do anything to protect, provide and parent your child. I kept Meredith safe from colds and earaches. I was extra careful to follow all the rules about getting her vaccinated, avoiding food that caused allergies and limiting her medications. My goal in life was to be Meredith's mom and I loved every minute of it.

Prior to this e-mail, Hunt and I had indeed been fighting the flu, but we also had been battling a bigger demon. Hunt had been physically and emotionally abusing me for four years. With the stress of our situation, the abuse became apparent to many people in our lives.

My admission to the hospital for preterm labor came at the worst time possible. We had just gotten through the Christmas season, which was always tough due to traveling and splitting the holidays between our families. We had invested in real estate, and that was taking a huge economic hit. And finally, Hunt's best friend was getting married. The perfect storm had hit our family, but the devastating surge had yet to arrive.

I was in the hospital for five days with preterm labor complications. My mother drove down from Virginia to take care of Meredith while I was recovering. Hunt and I struggled to get on the same page during this critical time. While he spent time with his best friend, I was meeting with a neonatologist to discuss the possibilities of having a premature, 3-pound baby. I felt that I needed my husband to be with me, but he felt differently. We argued over miscommunications and misplaced priorities, and he blamed my condition for his scheduling problems. I finally reached the point where I was done with Hunt. If he didn't want to be a part of saving our child's life, then I was done with him. But he wasn't done with me—or my family.

On January 17, our struggling marriage started to unravel under the pressure of our circumstances and the fractures in our relationship. Hunt received a phone call about a glitch in his best friend's upcoming wedding that made him boil with rage. It set in motion a ferocious argument between us and, since he could not explode at me in the hospital, he targeted my mother. He had always blamed my mother for my independent spirit, my strength, my lack of submission. He was dissatisfied with the way she had empowered me and made me the person I am. In his mind, she was to blame for the demise of our marriage. As he stormed out of my hospital room, he said he was going to our home, where my mother was caring for Meredith, and kicking her out. I tried unsuccessfully to warn her with a phone call. My family had no clue about this side of Hunt's personality. What my mother saw and my sick child endured that day, I never want to know in its entirety. I do know it was a vicious verbal attack by Hunt and his best friend, who arrived to participate in the ambush of my mother.

When my mother returned with Mer to see me at the hospital, I had never seen such a look of horror. She was extremely shaken and disturbed. I was not surprised at Hunt's behaviors at that point; after all, I had lived with this kind of madness for four years. But my family was starting to get a glimpse of the horrific temper I'd been dealing with. As I lay in the hospital bed, word traveled of Hunt's attack on my mother and the truth came out. My best friend—the only person aware of the abuse in my marriage—confirmed to my sister that this kind of assault was not unusual. My days of crying out in despair before the Lord were revealed. My family knew I had been physically and verbally beaten, and I was no longer going to live as I did.

The series of events that led up to Meredith's diagnosis of pediatric brain cancer are a blur. Hunt and I were officially separated after my hospitalization for preterm labor. He agreed to move out of our home, and my mother and I returned with Meredith and Tyler still in the womb. I will never forget how sick my little Meredith was. We believed she still had a touch of the flu. She was not eating, drinking her milk or doing much. She was obviously not herself.

The CT scan later revealed why she was so miserable—a tumor, looking to be the size of a golf ball, was growing at the base of her brain stem and obstructing the natural flow of fluid from her brain, causing hydrocephalus. It was also causing her brain to release a hormone that depletes sodium levels in her blood. Her blood work revealed that her sodium levels were low, which is caused by a condition called cerebral salt wasting. At the time we had no idea a tumor was making more of the hormone that controls water balance and causes the kidney to waste sodium in her urine. The doctor believed Meredith's tumor was most likely cancerous and had to be treated immediately. We'd have to move to Duke Hospital or Chapel Hill right away to get more information. I screamed in pain, I wept like I never had before. I stared at my baby lying there unconscious. This could not be happening to her, to me, to us. This news was devastating but I had no choice but to be strong.

What a gift it was for a bed to open at the Duke PICU for Meredith. I had no idea then how the staff members at this hospital would support and care for my child. Even though I was petrified as Meredith and I were transported by ambulance, I knew deep down that I was not alone. It was no coincidence that we lived close to one of the best hospitals in the country and that my daughter would be treated there.

My family and friends jumped into action, getting me clothes and a place to stay near the hospital, and spreading the word that Meredith needed a lot of prayer. She was scheduled for an MRI the next day, so we'd wait until then to see how serious her condition was.

Carepage Entry: Sunday, Jan. 27, 2008 10:17am

There have been so many loving e-mails and calls in the last few days. We really appreciate your thoughts and prayers. Unfortunately, our news has only gotten more devastating. We found out that Meredith has a brain tumor that has spread through her brain as well as her spinal fluid. It is quite an aggressive tumor with a poor outcome. The actual tumor portion came from the cerebellum side, but it is up against the brain stem. We are praying that it has not grown into the brain stem because they will not be able to get the entire tumor out.

There are two types of cancer that it could be; one is treatable and one is untreatable. If it is medulloblastoma, it is treatable with chemotherapy. If it is atypical teratoid rhabdoid tumor (AT/RT), a subcategory of medulloblastoma, it is untreatable. Meredith will still go into surgery to get an extraventricular drain (EVD) put into the top of her brain (to reduce the swelling from the hydrocephalus), and then they will remove the tumor as planned. The surgery will start after lunchtime (we've learned there is no pinpointing times in the hospital world). It will take about four to six hours, and then we will get to see her. They will watch her progress over the next few days, address whether she needs a permanent shunt to replace the EVD. The doctor said he has seen babies go home within a week, depending on their recovery. We will then wait a month to start chemotherapy.

All I can say is we need a miracle. Pray for a miracle. We are praying that God will heal Meredith fully. We will certainly have needs in the coming week, but right now we are staying in the hotel across the street from Duke, so our requests are limited. We haven't been home in days and have the hotel room booked until next Tuesday. There is nothing material that we need at this moment.

We are claiming Jeremiah 33:3, Isaiah 41:13 and Psalms 20:7. Please pray them with us as the Word of the Lord is sharper than a two-edged sword.

My Prayer: I call upon you Lord to show me great and mighty things. Although the fear of what You will reveal as Your will for my daughter's life is present, I know You will hold all of us in Your hands and will help us walk through this journey. I trust You even though I cannot see You. I feel Your physical touch through those you have sent to hold me. I will trust in You alone to heal my Meredith.

2

Raging Rivers

Carepage Entry: Tuesday, Jan. 29, 2008 10:19 a.m.

Well, we made it through our day, and we received some good news. I told God this morning that I wasn't strong enough for a bad report today. I just thought I might die. God was good and so was the pediatric neurosurgeon at Duke. Meredith went into surgery at 2:15 p.m., and at 3:30 p.m. they had put her drainage tube in place in the front of her head. From 3:30 to 6:30 p.m. they removed the tumor that is blocking her spinal fluid. We finally got to see her at 8 p.m. and she looked good. As far as the other tumors in her brain and spine, they are still unsure what type of cancer it is. We are believing that it is the treatable cancer, but we won't know for three or four days. They have to put the cells into formaldehyde and watch them over the next few days. We should know more on Thursday or Friday. Again, we appreciate all the people who have visited us in the hospital. Only immediate family will be allowed to see Meredith this week. There is so much sickness around and we cannot risk her getting anything during this critical time of recovery. We will definitely be at Duke till the middle of next week. I know so many of you want to do something, so rest up because when we get home we will need you in the following weeks if not months.

God has been so good to us through this crisis. We have Meredith for another day. If this tumor hadn't been caught at this time, I believe I would have walked in to get Meredith one morning and she would have gone to be with the Lord. We also have heard that there are churches and prayer groups praying for our little girl in North Carolina, Virginia, Florida and Arizona. I know every church in Raleigh, Knightdale, Clayton, and Rocky Mount has heard about Meredith and is praying. I've also realized just how many people really love our family. Wow, your outpouring of support and love has been amazing. God is good, I have been so blessed to have so many special friends love on me. Your encouragement has made a big difference in our lives.

Continue to pray that Meredith has the treatable cancer. How amazing would it be if Meredith was completely free of cancer when she gets her next MRI? A lady in the OR waiting room told me about her daughter, who had a form of cancer that turned into leukemia. She was told over and over by doctors that her child would not make it. She is now 14 years old. She gave me a new verse today that the Lord put on her heart years ago. It was from a part of the story of Jairus; He fell down at Jesus' feet and begged him to come to his house. He had only one daughter who lay dying. Jesus went to her and as her family grieved of her death, he said, "Do not be afraid; only believe and she will be *made well." (Luke 8:50, NASB). Jesus healed her. And so I believe that God's Word is truth and that my baby will too be healed. Thanks to all who have loved and supported us. Pray for our daughter every moment you can.*

Every day, we took turns sitting with Meredith. The days were long, tedious and emotional. I was wheeled into the hospital by my mother or my aunt. We stayed in the neonatal intensive care unit waiting room, while Hunt's family resided down the hall in the PICU waiting room. Our families tried not to speak because of the previous altercations. I was guarded from Hunt, and my activity was limited to the wheelchair or recliner next to Meredith. I was not supposed to get up, and I had to drink a ton of water and take Nifedipine every three hours to avoid going into labor. Tyler was one insistent baby. I could detect a contraction as soon as the medicine wore off.

It was during these long hours of waiting, praying and greeting visitors that I began divulging all my marital garbage. I will never forget my mother taking notes on everything I said and my aunt asking question after question to extract every detail. I know they were trying to comprehend all that I was saying. I was an open book. All of the secrets, all of my realities were exposed. My mother was amazing. As a mother myself, I cannot imagine listening to my own child recount all the abusive behaviors I endured. I am grateful that she just listened and supported me. I was so ready to release all of those hidden stories and to be free of the secrets that had consumed my life.

My family responded by building a fortress around me. They were shocked and their anger burned deeply. During this time I was in a wheelchair, Hunt would often ask if he could talk with me privately. My family was reluctant to leave me alone with him but I agreed to talk. I suppose I wanted him to say something that would turn back time and change all of his abusive behavior, but an apology wasn't enough anymore. I had heard so many meaningless and fruitless words. The proof would be in his behavior.

I simply could not give him the emotional energy required to deal with my broken marriage. I needed to focus on the two crises before me. I asked Hunt to wait until Meredith was stable and Tyler was 36 weeks before I gave him an answer on whether or not our marriage would be salvageable. This infuriated him. It fueled his frustration and caused even greater strife between us.

I felt so much disappointment. I had to carry on, though. God was not taking me over this battle, but through it. I just had to believe that our marriage could be dealt with later. My focus was on my son and my daughter and their health and safety. They were all I could think about and all I wanted to think about.

Carepage Entry: Wednesday, Jan. 30, 2008 8:00 p.m.

First of all, thank you for your many e-mails, calls, gifts and visits. You would not believe the number of e-mails I am getting from people all over the United States. One e-mail was from a mother whose child was diagnosed with a tumor around the brain stem and got news similar to ours, but is now 16 years old. Oh, how I need to hear of all these miracles. I know God can do anything, but it is so hard to keep believing when you watch your child suffer. I feel so weak, but God is giving me enough strength to get through each day and to make decisions I never fathomed I would be making. Every night I keep thinking...how did I survive this day? How did my baby survive today? How can our families keep helping while grieving? All I can say is it is supernatural, unexplainable, unbelievable.

As far as an update on our little girl, today was a better day. Meredith has had trouble focusing with her eyes; she has nystagmus from the surgery. This is just rapid eye movement—she is looking to the left and center, but not the right. We saw this yesterday, but it is somewhat normal and seems to be getting better. Her spinal fluid is draining well—the doctor was encouraged. The pediatric neurosurgeons are still assessing whether or not she needs a shunt to drain fluid off of her brain. We are praying she will not need one because it means more surgery, more recovery time and more time before we can start chemotherapy. Meredith also cannot move her right leg. As devastating as this sounds, I believe it will get better too. The doctor thinks the tumors in her spine are pushing on the nerves in that leg. Just as her eyes are getting better we are expecting her leg to, as well.

The pathologist report has not come back, but I have a feeling we will get it tomorrow (Thursday). Oh, how the fear creeps in each time I think of hearing the results. It is the most frightening thing to think about. Pray for peace. We need to feel God's hands around us when we sit at that conference table with Meredith's doctors. When you think of us tomorrow, pray specifically for these things: the cancer is treatable; there is no need for a shunt; Meredith heals quickly from surgery; and that she feels no pain, only peace.

Yesterday, a wonderful friend gave me a card with the most beautiful poem:

I come to the swift, raging river.
And the roar held the echo of fear;
"Dear Lord, give me the wings to fly over,
If you are, as promised, quite near."

*But He said "Trust the grace I am giving,
All pervasive, sufficient for you.
Take my hand—we will face this together,
But my plan is—not over, but through."
(Unknown Author)*

*We are facing the swiftest and scariest raging river, and
I thank God that He is with us to pull us through. I know
one day we will look back at this experience and we will
NOT ask "why us?" but we will say "use us."*

My mind and body were on autopilot. My goals were to
keep my son inside of me and to watch my daughter like a
hawk for abnormal behaviors. I watched hours and hours
for any changes in her breathing, coughing or movement.
I was trying to outsmart the cancer. I hoped my efforts could
save her from pain or fear.

Cancer is tricky and deceitful. Just when you think you
are smarter, stronger and more powerful, it outwits you.
Yes, I thought I could help her, and I did as much as I could.
But, ultimately, I was helpless. I had no power against this
cancer. The only thing I could do was plead before God
to save her. I begged, I believed and I worried. I cried and
screamed. God knew I would do anything to keep her, for
her to be well again. He knew I would dedicate my life to
serving her if she had brain damage. He knew I would
fight for her to be treated fairly and I would give her a
good life. But I read the stories of other children who have
battled medulloblastoma. So many fight it for years and,
just when the treatments end, the sneaky cells reappear.
They are unmerciful and seek to destroy.

I believed that God could heal Meredith. I knew He
was capable of changing Mer's fate, but I remember
saying multiple times, "I know that He <u>can</u> do it, but I don't

know if He <u>will</u> do it for Meredith." The thing is, I knew God had a plan. I knew that He wanted what was best for my baby. However, it was hard to accept the possibility that she would not be healed.

In the midst of my struggles, God was there. What I wanted was for Him to kill Meredith's cancer and to protect me from my husband and his family's verbal assaults. Why wasn't He stopping the abuse? Wasn't I enduring enough, watching my child suffer from an aggressive cancer? Didn't they know that any stress could put me back into premature labor?

I do believe with all of my heart that God was holding my hand throughout this journey. He rescued me from so much and defended me when necessary. My family and friends were like a barbed-wire fence that surrounded me. They were there to love me, hold me, cry with me, protect me and defend me. When the enemy came on strong, which he did daily, they took over half the burden and carried it for me. In the midst of all of these struggles, God was there.

My Prayer: God, I know you were with me during these trials, but not in the way that I envisioned. There were no breaks for me, and I was so weary. I felt Your presence and heard Your voice, Lord, but it was faint compared to the angry voices around me. My desire was for You to give me the wings to fly over my raging rivers, but it seemed You wanted me to take Your hand and go through.

3

War

We continue to be touched by everyone's care and concern during this time. All of your encouragement has been helpful to get through each day. Yesterday was a very difficult day for us all. I am clinging to this verse this morning as I write this: "Weeping may endure for the night, but a shout of joy comes in the morning." (Psalm 30:5, NASB).

Oh, there were a lot of tears shed yesterday; mine were much needed since I hadn't cried for the last two days. As many of you know, I am not the most patient person and, although I am quickly learning that the medical world could care less about that, they are also learning that I am not the type who is going to sit back and wait. My breaking point came yesterday at 7 p.m. Our family was under the impression that the pathology report was going to be back yesterday morning, so we were there at 6:30 a.m. to make sure we didn't miss the doctor. He was encouraging about Meredith's other issues, but the report was not back. Around 2:30 p.m., the pressure in Meredith's brain was increasing, so her EVD tube started leaking and she threw up and seemed a little uncomfortable. Things started becoming alarming to me. We assumed labs would be back after 3 p.m. and at 5 p.m., when we had not heard from anyone, we started pressing for answers. We also hadn't heard anything from the neurology team about the leak in her head. They did take her down for a "STAT CT scan," which ended up taking two hours. I guess if you're scheduled for a regular CT scan that means you wait for days. While she is the scan, we found out that the lab "mis-stained" Meredith's tissues and they would need to be re-stained on Monday.

After the CT scan, things began to get worse. I had that same feeling I had at WakeMed when everyone kept saying "that's normal, she's making progress, etc.," and I knew in my soul, body and heart that things were not okay. A mother's intuition was very powerful and, frankly, last night that is what it was. I don't need a medical degree to know when my baby is acting normal or not—I'm sure many of you can relate. Well, I had to hyperventilate and demand medical attention and basically make a scene, but I did get my baby seen and I have a feeling I won't have to wait to see a doctor 4.5 hours again.

It ends up that pressure in Meredith's brain increased yesterday and they had to reopen the extra ventricular drain (EVD) to let spinal fluid drain out. This means that we are not in the clear for the shunt. The scan showed more fluid in her brain, so we basically have to start over with increasing pressure using the tube and seeing if she can move the fluid through her spine. After the EVD was reactivated, she perked up and began eating again and feeling better.

My sister, two aunts and Mama 2 (my grandmother) did the night shift last night and sure enough that Psalm above rang true. They said she had a great night, she slept a lot and my sister held her for two hours and my aunt held her the next three. She got great sleep. There are two things Meredith lives for—to be held and to be held. She's always been a cuddle bug.

So today is going to be a better day. I feel at peace and will probably stay at the hotel for a while. I am so emotionally exhausted and I feel like I've been run over by an 18-wheeler. It wears me out to watch Meredith hour after hour in that bed. It's so baffling when just over two weeks ago she was crawling, pulling up, laughing and throwing all her food off her highchair to our dog. Wow, how things can change in the blink of an eye. Cherish everything your child does, no matter how crazy or annoying it is. Every ounce of me yearns to see her yelling at me through the gate to let her out so she could eat a piece of paper off the floor or just follow me around. One day that will happen again.

Sitting in Duke Hospital, watching my daughter struggle to stay alive, was the most terrifying experience of my life. As soon as Meredith's personality was revealed to me, I knew she would be the CEO of a business. She was not a follower, she was a doer. I had so many dreams for her, but as I looked at her bruised and frail body, I knew her future included brain surgery, a shunt, a port and then chemotherapy. This was not only the fight of her life, but it was also mine. At the time, I thought for sure I would die with my daughter. This war against cancer would result in two deaths if we did not succeed. I just knew I could not live without my little girl. I shed so many tears as I struggled to hang onto to hope.

God gave me enough strength each day to survive the horrific realities and battles that I faced. I don't know about you, but I often have my most desperate times with the Lord while I am in the shower. There is something about being in a tight, white place with scalding hot water beating down that brings me closer to the Lord. During this time, I spent my mornings on the bathtub floor praying for strength, begging for a miracle and asking, "why?" I do the same thing now as I prepare for my day. I go to God in complete desperation each morning and beg for His peace and provision. I am not going to tell you that He answers me the way I want each time I leave this place of solitude, but at least I know I have given my hopes and fears to Him.

Carepage Entry: Feb. 5, 2008 8:16 a.m.

The pathology report arrived tonight and finally we have some good news! Meredith has a treatable cancer, medulloblastoma. Duke and St. Jude have been working together to create a successful protocol for this type of cancer. Meredith's neurosurgeon confirmed there have been many successful cases. He was optimistic and we were so grateful.

So many other things happened today that prepared us for this news. Meredith had a terrible night, but a great day. She was sleeping peacefully today and, when she was awake, she didn't fuss unless she was hungry. She also ate a lot; she seemed a little more like herself. For those of you who know Meredith, you will be able to visualize this: Today she was trying to rip off the heart monitor stickers as well as the EVD in her head. *She definitely has a feisty side to her (I wonder where she got that?).*

So, we had a very good day. I felt hopeless and totally numb as I got ready to go to the hospital this morning. I have been very depressed the last two days. I felt my prayers were not really working. I prayed that God would give me something to hold on to today—some good news, some comfort and some peace. About midday, I felt an overwhelming peace that carried me through talks with a variety of doctors as well as hours of waiting. God also gave me a gift of being with Meredith all day. I had enough energy to care for her in every way. I truly miss caring for my little girl like I used to. I miss carrying her around the house, going to the grocery store with her in the cart, seeing her cute little face screaming in her crib every time I try to blow-dry my hair in the mornings (just to name a few things). I cannot wait for those days to come once again.

Another concern has been Meredith's need for a shunt. We pretty much accepted that she would be getting one this evening or tomorrow morning. Her spinal fluid output was 190 ml on Sunday morning and 170 ml this morning. Normal is 100 ml. We figured there was no way it would get down to 100 in one day, so we scheduled the shunt for tomorrow at 10 a.m. We also planned for the chemotherapy port to be put in at the same time. This shunt will drastically change the approach of the chemotherapy as we were hoping Meredith could get an Ommaya reservoir (a device placed under the scalp through which chemotherapy can be administered directly to the central nervous system). However, the shunt will prevent her from getting the Ommaya, so the port in her chest is the second best option. It was a big deal. When I had the nurse check at 4 p.m. today, Meredith had only produced 40 ml of *fluid. After you do the math that comes to 90-100 ml at 7 a.m. tomorrow. I was thrilled by the news and knew it would truly be a miracle if she was in the normal range tomorrow morning. But I believe that Meredith will continue to absorb that fluid tonight! It would be so awesome for her to avoid that surgery. We will just have to wait till morning to see!*

I have much more to say but I am so exhausted! I will have to write again tomorrow evening. Please pray for these things:

1. *Her spinal fluid is close to 100 ml tomorrow morning.*
2. *If she is supposed to get a shunt, it will be done tomorrow so she can go home by the weekend.*
3. *If she is going to have surgery, it will be successful and done skillfully.*
4. *We will have peace when we meet with the oncology team and learn what the chemo protocol will be.*
5. *A pain-free day.*

Thank you for all of your prayers. They are working and will continue to carry us through this time.

Fighting cancer is like fighting a war. I believe that fighting cancer calls for a warlike mentality. Being in a hospital is like being in a foreign country. The battle is against an evil and powerful enemy that threatens to destroy your innocence and freedom. The fight calls for sacrifice—if not by you, then by another. Let me explain my thought about the foreign land. When your child has cancer, you are torn from your home and you begin living in a hospital. The staff members try to comfort you and make you feel at home, but the reality is you're in a hospital and your child is gravely ill. Once you acclimate to the beeping machines, medicine rituals, continuous interruptions, bad food and dirty restrooms, you then begin the fight of your life. I imagine that a soldier endures similar disorientation when adjusting to a new location after being deployed.

As I looked around this new home, I realized it was the real thing. I wasn't watching a family beg for money to cure cancer on the St. Jude telethon. I was living it. I tried to make the best of my situation by making Meredith's crib entertaining. I watched some TV and entertained visitors, but in the back of my mind I was trying to figure out how my child would ever be free from this cancer. Its devastation churned within my soul. Then, I began to think about the consequences of brain surgery and chemotherapy, and I knew it would be an absolute miracle if my little one beat this monster. The questions were constant. Will she ever have a full life? What more can I do to save her? Will she be normal again? Quitting was not an option—we'd come too far and I was willing to sacrifice everything, even my life, if only she would live.

The bargaining and wrestling would turn into begging. Finally, I'd realize that when God gave me this child at conception there was a possibility He would want her back. I'd beg God to take me instead. I would take the brain cancer and all its horrifying consequences if only she would be made well. I'd sacrifice anything and give Him everything if only He would change His plans right then and there. Ultimately, I had to honor the commitment I made when God placed her in my womb and I said, "She is Yours."

2 Timothy 2:3 says, "Endure hardship with us like a good soldier of Christ Jesus." It is tricky to march on when cancer invades your life and takes you to a place of so much fear and trauma. In war, soldiers encounter unimaginably horrific sights that they struggle to leave behind. I have

my own memories of battle that play again and again. I see on Meredith's body wounds of war from surgery, the paralysis of her limbs from the cancer cells in her spine, the agony on her face when nurses take blood for the fiftieth time. I see my baby girl breathing so fast it seems her heart and lungs might explode. I hear the doctor suggest that I need to think about whether I want to shock her if her heart fails. I feel the embrace of loved ones who don't know what to say to me. I see my mom's face when she tells me, "Beth, she is going to be okay. It is okay, Beth. We are just going to pray." Yes, those memories of 2008 will plague me forever.

In the United States, we have so many advantages with our medical technologies, amazing surgeons and nurses, and chemotherapy protocols. But the outcome is always up to God and His plan for our lives and, in the midst of so much suffering, God gives hope and abundant blessings. "Beth, hold on, she is more than just okay, she is healed." Love, God.

Carepage Entry: Feb. 7, 2008 1:08 p.m.

I know it has been days since I've sent out an update, but things have been so crazy for us this week. Last time I wrote, Meredith was not looking like she'd need a shunt, but it appears that's the direction we're going at this time. She was scheduled to have surgery tomorrow to put in a shunt and a port for the chemo, but we found out last night she has an infection where the tubing is and we will not be able to do the shunt until that clears up. So she is having surgery to replace the EVD tubing and put in the port today at 3 p.m. Then, they will watch her and step up the antibiotics to get rid of the infection. Because this cancer is an aggressive one, the oncologist wants to start chemo as soon as the neurosurgeon clears Meredith. This infection is a setback for us in a big way. Now she has to have two surgeries instead of one, and the infection has to be gone; plus, she has to recover from the shunt surgery. Her neurosurgeon said he wants her to recover for at least one week. The oncologist wants to start two days after surgery. I was hoping to bring Mer home for a few days between surgery and chemo, but it looks like that will not be a possibility. We are on the waiting list at the Ronald McDonald House, so we are hoping to move there this week.

After spending the night at the hospital last night, I felt so discouraged. Meredith had a really bad night of coughing and discomfort. Your Carepage messages have been very encouraging, but nothing compares to God's Word. I've told the Lord that Meredith is His and I will honor whatever He decides for her. He loves her more than I do and He already knows the outcome. I will not allow each setback to weaken my faith. I might be physically and mentally depleted, but spiritually I am made strong by His constant touch.

When I arrived back to the hotel this morning, my mom encouraged me to read my devotional. This was the verse God gave me to get through this day: "I will bless the Lord at all times; His praise shall continually be in my mouth."(Psalm 34:1, NASB).

God has brought my daughter through brain surgery, heavy-duty medications, extreme pain and discomfort, and many other things this week. I praise Him for that and continue to look for the little miracles as well as the big ones each and every day.

Thank you again for your love and support. Today I received an e-mail from a soldier in Iraq, and he assured *me that Baghdad was now in prayer for my sweet baby. Wow, God continues to show that the world isn't such a big place after all.*

The Psalms are full of inspiration, desperation and redemption. Psalm 84:5-7 pretty much sums up my life. "Blessed are those whose strength is in you, who have set their hearts of pilgrimage. As they pass though the valley of Baca, they make it a place of springs; the autumn rains also cover it with pools. They go from strength to strength until each appears before God in Zion." It is almost unreal to think that there will be blessings at the end of my pilgrimage. I mean, I know that God's Word is true. But fighting against cancer, fear, abandonment is overwhelming. I cannot see the rest stops and, where I do stop, the water fountains are germy. I believe, though, and I have to keep on going. As Beth Moore (2008) says, "If God had already taken us everywhere He intended, we'd be at His glorious feet by now." God has a lot more for me to do.

My Prayer: My past cannot be changed, but my future certainly has been altered beyond belief. Lord, I beg You to show me the way. Help me to be obedient no matter how afraid and fragile I feel. Give me the vigor to fulfill my destiny. Don't let my pain paralyze me. Give me the strength I need to praise You in the midst of my daughter's suffering.

4

The Blessings of Birth

Carepage Entry: Feb. 18, 2008 9:36 a.m.

How unbelievable is it that my two babies were born almost exactly one year apart? Yes, Tyler was born on Feb. 15, 2008, one day before Meredith's first birthday. He weighed 6 pounds, 5 ounces and was 19 inches long. I had him at 4:29 in the morning. We love you and appreciate all the prayers, flowers and gifts.

I absolutely love telling people the story behind Tyler's birth. It was such a God thing! Mom and I went to my obstetrician for a check Feb. 6 and I was frantic about Meredith because she was getting a MRI later that day. As I was lying on the examining table waiting for my doctor, I turned over and felt wetness on the paper cloth. I had a complete panic attack and started screaming, "My water broke! I cannot have this baby right now!" Mom quickly said, "Beth calm down, it could be urine." I responded in haste, "Mom, it is NOT urine. I would have known if I peed on myself!" At that time, the nurse and doctor rushed in and examined me. They confirmed that it was not amniotic fluid. The doctor said, "I think you need something to help with your anxiety."

On Feb. 13, I went to the obstetrician for another check and this time I was leaking amniotic fluid. The midwife suggested I go to the hospital and get checked in. I told her I was not going because Meredith was having surgery on the 14th or 15th. She was scheduled to get a shunt for her hydrocephalus and a port for upcoming chemotherapy treatments. My doctor agreed to add one more dose of Nifedipine to stop the contractions. I laughed all the way back to Duke Hospital and kept saying to myself, "There is no way I am going to have this baby right now." I had to take my medicine every three hours, setting timers to stay on schedule.

On Feb. 15, Mom, Mama 2 and I were in the hotel room sleeping. My Aunt Joyce Lynne arrived around 1:30 a.m., and I woke up to take my Nifedipine. I went to the restroom, sat back on the bed and felt a gush of water. I yelled, "Oh my gosh! My water just broke." My aunt jumped up and said, "Okay, let's go have a baby." Mom insisted I go get a shower while they all got ready. My water was leaking everywhere and I wasn't sure how I was supposed to keep from getting drenched, so Mama 2 spoke up and said, "You can wear one of my Depends." I embraced the idea! Joyce Lynne went and got the car, and we all piled in.

Meredith was scheduled for surgery at 8 a.m. Since my last OB appointment, I had set up an emergency team in case I did go into labor early. My dad and sister were to go to the hospital with Meredith, and mom, my birthing coach, had to be with me. The timing of the birth was unique. My best friend had spent the day before getting me a new doctor at Duke. I was supposed to call and set up an appointment with this new practice immediately. Not to mention, this was the day before Meredith's first birthday.

My 86-year-old grandmother, Joyce Lynne, mom and I all chuckled as we drove 45 minutes from Duke Hospital in Durham to WakeMed in Raleigh. I think we were just laughing at the outlandish circumstances. Here we are practically living at Duke but were heading to a different hospital in another city. My aunt went on and on about how amazed she was that we had no traffic. It certainly was a blessing that my labor started in the middle of the night since a daytime trip from Durham to Raleigh would have taken over an hour. It was clear that God had laid out a perfect plan for us that night.

One thing was for sure, I had to have a VBAC (vaginal birth after cesarean). There was no time to recover from another C-section. My doctor's practice was one of few that offered a VBAC, so going to Raleigh was really the only option. As we drove my contractions were about 10 minutes apart. When we got to the hospital and settled in at 2:45 a.m., I was 6 cm. My contractions were picking up then, and my obstetrician and nurse arrived to ask if I wanted an epidural. I was undecided because the pains were not bad right then, so I looked at Mom and she said, "You are doing fine." The nurse concurred, and we were off to the delivery room, where my grandmother and aunt were waiting. I was in some pain, nothing unbearable. But it all went south quickly when I reached 8 cm and my contractions came every three minutes. Mom was by my side, trying to get me to breathe, but I just couldn't get it together. When it was time to push I was clueless. I never had the urge to push, so I had to bear down with all my might. I started to scream and Mom said, "Why are you screaming? Does it hurt? Pushing isn't supposed to hurt; it's supposed to feel good." My obstetrician said he thought my family could hear me in Durham. He decided to give me a nerve block to help with the pain. The physical pain was intense, but it paled in comparison to the emotional pain I was feeling over Meredith. I could see my aunt in the background cheering and my grandmother praying in the chair. I pushed five times and Tyler arrived into this world!

Hunt did not attend Tyler's birth, and that turned out to be a relief. Three generations of my family were there for him. My grandmother, mom and aunt are three of the most influential women in my life. It was an honor to have them present as I gave birth to the child who would give me joy in times when it seemed unattainable. My birthing team was amazing, and the peace and love in that room eased my soul as I remembered I would not be present at a critical moment in Meredith's battle with cancer.

The day of Tyler's birth was filled with many visitors and constant phone updates from my family on Meredith's surgery and recovery. There was numbness around me, what I consider God's protection, as Meredith's status remained serious. Although her surgery was successful she was still in critical condition. She was so sick and my family was trying to keep me in the dark. As I lay in that bed incapable of helping, my dad came to visit and I asked him, "Is she going to die?" He just cried and left the room. I don't know how I made it through that day. I wasn't panicked as I knew God would not let my girl die when I was not there. I knew she would make it through the night, so that I could celebrate her first birthday with her.

Carepage Entry: Feb. 18, 2008 9:36 a.m.

On Saturday I got to hold Meredith for four hours straight! My doctors at WakeMed gave me a pass to leave for eight hours so I could go to Duke for Mer's birthday. It felt amazing to hold her again comfortably. That little guy in my stomach made it very difficult to hold her last week. So I am grateful to finally have a lap! Meredith also opened her eyes and looked at me today. What an awesome gift that was. I hadn't seen her eyes in three days. It was a wonderful moment. Today was a very good day; it was so good to see Meredith making some progress. Today we start chemotherapy and hopefully we will see some good things occur immediately. Please continue to pray for our little patient to get stronger and stronger each day. She is going to need strength and endurance for the week ahead. Pray for peace for each of us as well.

So that was the beginning of my little boy's life. He was flexible and eager to see the world from the very start. I think it is very interesting that God planned Tyler's birth the day before Meredith's birthday. The timing was so unique. At the time, it didn't seem so good. The logistics of Tyler's arrival seemed overwhelming, but God reminded me that some of His greatest blessings don't come in the simplest of packages.

My prayer: Lord, Tyler is truly a gift from above. Thank you for bringing him into my life at the most perfect time. Thank you for allowing me to feel joy in the midst of deep grief and sorrow. Help me not to be anxious about today or tomorrow. Impress upon my heart the necessity to rejoice in this moment of new life. "And we know that all things work together for good to them that love God." (Romans 8:28).

5
Held

Carepage Entry: Feb. 21, 2008 4:10 p.m.

Today my mother and I spent the entire morning with Meredith. It was a really peaceful day. Her labs look good. The doctors are keeping a close eye on her sodium levels as well as her white blood cell counts. She has tolerated the chemo well. Our oncologist confirmed yesterday that Meredith is in a coma. We guessed this might be the case but we chose to believe she was sleeping. It is reality. Her pupils no longer dilate and her only way of communicating is through her vital signs. This state is due to the pressure on her brain from the tumors. We are praying fervently that one round of chemo will alleviate some of this pressure so she can wake up. Hearing that your daughter is in coma is definitely a shock. I cannot even describe the feeling that wells up when I try to comprehend this. I keep envisioning Meredith at Christmas crawling around playing with our family dog's bone. She could have cared less about her new clothes and toys. She just wanted to play with dog toys. I guess it's only fair considering he rips the eyes off her stuffed animals. Anyway, it is truly unbelievable that a month and a half ago our baby was just like every other 11-month-old and now she is fighting for her life.

I have no regrets with Meredith. She was spoiled by all who loved her and I thank God for it! I put this verse on Meredith's birth announcement, and it is so true: "Lo, children are a heritage of the Lord; and the fruit of the womb is His reward." (Psalm 127:3, KJV).

I believe and am claiming that Meredith is in a "heavenly coma." If she was awake, she would surely be in pain and agitated. It would be more difficult to get through the days watching her cry. I believe that God is holding her in His hands right now, protecting her from the pain of these tumors.

The next 10 days are crucial for Meredith. The chemo will be working and a lot of things can happen. She will be very susceptible to infection because her white blood cell counts will be very low. It is critical that she is protected from the flu, colds, etc. We've made a list of the immediate family who can see Meredith; the fewer people who visit her, the better. We know many of you would like to see Mer, but it's critical that we protect her by restricting visitors. If you would like to see Hunt, Tyler or me, just give us a call before coming. Hunt and I are on different schedules— I usually stay with Meredith all day and he sits with her after work. Feel free to call, though, so we can work out a way to see you. Again, we appreciate your visits, but the BEST thing you can do is to PRAY. There has been talk about fasting different things for Meredith until she's healed, and that's definitely something we'd love for you to pray about. Whatever God lays on your heart to do would be great. We have no expectations and just appreciate anything you can do to help.

Tyler is doing great. He is getting up hungry every three hours. He is growing and is just as cute as can be. He has the same mouth and chin as Meredith. I think the rest of him looks like me!

I was deeply touched by those who loved me during this time. While Meredith was resting peacefully in her heavenly coma, my mom and I moved out of the Brentwood Inn into the Ronald McDonald House. It was truly a privilege to get in so quickly, but I was used to living in a hotel right at the hospital so that in a moment's notice I could be there for Meredith. I was so thankful that we were able to stay close for so long. Even though I was scared to move to the RMH, it was time.

The Ronald McDonald House alleviated some of the financial burden my parents were carrying. Even though my Bible study friends and former workplace had sent me money, it was not feasible to stay. Plus, the RMH provided my family with support and protection. I remember crying as I walked in the first time. I was scared of what things lay ahead. It seemed so final, like this nightmare was going to last a long time. I wanted to go back home. Then I had the sobering thought that even if we could go home, we really did not have one to return to.

The fact was Hunt and I were rarely together anymore because we were separated. After many apologies and empty promises, I could not bring myself to recommit to this marriage. I needed Meredith to be out of crisis before I could make decisions about our future. As a result, Hunt emptied our bank accounts, locked me out of the house and confiscated all of my journals and personal documents, leaving me with no way to support myself. My parents, extended family and friends equipped me emotionally, spiritually, physically, financially and mentally. Hunt had consumed my life for the last four years. He pulled me away from almost everyone--- except my best friend, by God's grace! I am amazed at the way God brought light into darkness during that time. He provided me with family members and friends who gave me clarity. For the first time, I accepted that I had been abused, and I became stronger. I had been completely abandoned by Hunt but not by God.

God held Meredith, Tyler and me so closely. I will never forget feeling His peace in the most frightening times of my life. Even though I was at a loss over my marriage, God gave me a clear focus—my children. Meredith and Tyler were the most important people to me. Nothing could cloud my focus. I had to give them everything I had.

> To think that providence
> Would take a child from his mother
> While she prays, is appalling
> Who told us we'd be rescued
> What has changed and
> Why should we be saved from nightmares
> We're asking why this happens to us
> Who have died to live, it's unfair
>
> This is what it means to be held
> How it feels, when the sacred is torn from your life
> And you survive
> This is what it is to be loved and to know
> That the promise was when everything fell
> We'd be held

Wells, C. (2005)

My Prayer: Lord, help to feel your arms around me. Give me the faith and hope that I need to focus on Your glory versus my circumstances. Romans 8:18 (NASB) says the "sufferings of this present time are not worthy to be compared with the glory that is to be revealed to us," but my suffering is nearly suffocating me. Remind me of Your promises and as I trade all that I thought was stable and true for a new normal, please never let go.

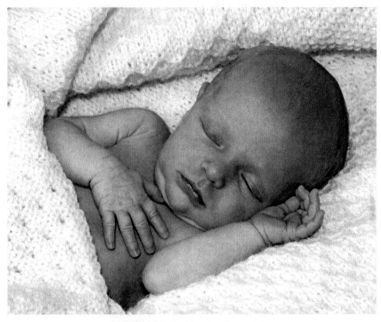

Meredith: 2 weeks old

Meredith and Mommy: 2 weeks old

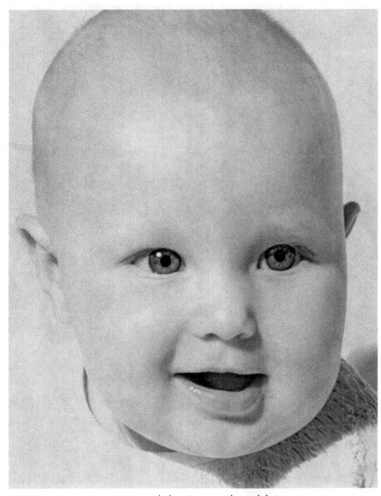

Meredith: 6 months old

Meredith: 6 months old

Tyler: 9 months old

Tyler and Mommy: 9 months old

6
Return to Me

Carepage Entry: Feb. 29, 2008 1:18 p.m.

I am currently sitting next to my Sleeping Beauty, who looks as peaceful and perfect as she did when she was well. When I look at Meredith I visualize all the tubes and scars gone, and I just see my gorgeous baby. Not to brag, but everyone always thought she was so pretty, they even say that now with all the swelling and wires. She is one of a kind!

The last two days we have been able to breathe because Mer has been resting comfortably. What an answer to prayer! The first night she was in the step-down unit, which provides care for patients who need less monitoring than those in the PICU, we had a crisis. Meredith's belly became distended and they had to put an additional tube down her nose to get out the air and irritation. It was very scary and has changed some of the chemo plans, but she has recovered and is working hard to stay strong. We have seen some little but very promising changes this week. Her legs definitely have some tension when we do her PT exercises. We are elated to see any movement because her right leg has not moved since the very first surgery. Her eyes are also dilating, but they are all over the place. However, today she has been able to keep them somewhat in sync. We don't know how much she can see, but she is responsive to our voices. Meredith has also been making a few sounds, especially when we move her around. So, overall we are seeing good progress. Her doctor says that we are still not "out of the woods" but, as we all know, God can do anything. We believe Meredith will burst out of those "woods" when God gives her the go!

We have been so blessed to have great doctors and nurses. One of Meredith's nurses in the Pediatric Intensive Care Unit was such a miracle worker. I cried when she left us in step-down. She came by to see Meredith today and we expressed how much she meant to us and how we missed her. I want to buy her a car or something to show my gratitude. When I left for the evenings and Mer was in her care, I knew she would treat my little one the way I would. She watched her every move and never got tired of my questions, no matter how silly or serious they were. I am continually amazed at how God provides for Meredith and for me at every moment. It is not by chance or by luck that we got to Duke or that Mer's surgeons are some of the best in the world or that her pediatric oncologist has helped save many children with this cancer. God is in control, He knew exactly what we would need and HE has provided. No one else will get the credit, ever!

Today, we were lucky to get a wonderful nurse, who is a Christian. She encouraged me this morning by telling me about another little girl who had medulloblastoma and she had gone through the same crisis and challenges with her. She is at home now and comes to visit the nurses when she comes for chemo. She reminded me that God can do anything even when we have no hope and things look grim. How I needed that little bit of encouragement today. Thank you Lord for giving me enough to get through each day!

Thank you to all who are going out of your way to provide and pray for us. We are so grateful. Continue to pray for Meredith's body to recover from her first round of chemo. Also, for her white blood cell counts to come up. They are at their lowest and we expect to see them come up by day 12 of the cycle (Sunday). And, of course, pray for a miracle to occur.

Meredith was getting better and I was so grateful. I was encouraged and hopeful. God was speaking to me in so many ways. I felt Him and saw the work of His hands as all my needs were met by the body of Christ. However, Meredith wasn't a miracle yet. We had a long way to go.

Meredith's sickness was the catalyst that pushed me closer to God. I had never heard from the Lord till Meredith was brought into my life. In the past, I knew He had led me to make right decisions and showed me the way in certain situations, but Meredith propelled me to seek God in an entirely different way. Formally, my walk with the Lord was controlled by rules and feelings of obligation; now it was out of desperation to know Him deeply and a desire to be ONE with Him. I began searching for the hidden meaning behind costly circumstances and wanting to know the mind of Christ, His power and His peace. Meredith made me yearn to be more than just a mom, a teacher and a friend. Meredith inspired me to be a woman of purpose, change and encouragement. Although the pain of watching her suffer was excruciating, I knew that it would one day be used for God's glory.

Carepage Entry: March 2, 2008 2:46 pm.

Where do I begin? God is good, all the time! Today when I saw Meredith I wept with joy. She looks so good— the best she has looked in weeks. Her white blood cell counts are up from .2 to 4 today (normal is 10-15). We are expecting them to continue to come up through the week. She is crying out more. We believe this is her way of communicating with us. I never thought I would be thankful to hear Meredith cry. It used to make me crazy and now it's like sweet music to my ears. It feels so good to hear her make any sound.

Yesterday I had been so discouraged. Meredith was resting peacefully, but sometimes it seems more difficult to watch nothing happen than have a crisis. The days seem endless in the hospital; it is like time stands still. When I went home yesterday, I just stood in Mer's room in agony. I know so many good things are coming from this experience, but the "human" side of me doesn't care. All I want is my baby back. I want to see her smile, hear her say "Ma, Ma," watch her crawl around the house. Then, God reminds me that this is all part of my story, my walk and my journey through life. I can make it through anything with Him. He is walking beside me, holding my precious baby in His hands. I feel grateful to have those memories of Meredith and I know I will have more in the future.

I have been lifted up by all of your prayers and e-mails. One individual said, "God is still in the business of miracles." Yes, what a good reminder. Also, when my Mom, Joyce Lynne and I were out to eat this weekend, our waiters were seminary students from Southeastern Theological Seminary in Wake Forest, N.C. They wrote down Mer's name and offered to pray for her. Wow. I have been blown away by the body of Christ. How powerful God's people are when they unite!

Thank you for taking the time to pray for our family. We are claiming that Meredith will come through this disease and will be completely restored.

God was giving me the people in my life that I needed to get through these trials, and it looked like He might be giving me a healed child. I would just have to wait and see. It was such a blessing to feel so much love and support and to see positive progress with Meredith's health. I was cautiously optimistic, and extremely driven. I wanted Meredith to get the best care available, which meant being her advocate. God continued to give me focus. I was challenged with Joel 2:12: "Even now, declares the Lord, return to me with all your heart, with fasting and weeping and mourning." I had spent my life "returning to" the things of this world, but God wanted me to return to Him.

My Prayer: Lord, I know you are the only One that I can return to. I am crying at Your feet and begging for comfort as You know my pain like no other. Inspire me to continue giving myself to You minute by minute. Lead me through this wilderness into a land flowing with milk and honey, just as You have promised me. (Deuteronomy 6:3).

7

Miracle Meredith

Carepage Entry: March 6, 2008 10:07 a.m.

Miracle Meredith! Praise God!!!!!! We are elated to tell you that Meredith had an MRI yesterday and, not only have the tumors stopped growing, but they are SHRINKING!!!! Thank you, Lord! Thank you, God! It is a miracle. Meredith's pediatric neuro-oncologist told us it can take 10 weeks to see a difference in the tumors, but here we are after less than three weeks of treatment and he can see progress. He'll show me the results this afternoon but he wanted tell me the good news before he came.

Never underestimate the power of prayer and the power of our almighty God! We asked and He has answered! Thank you so much for your dedication to my daughter. I am so grateful! I will write another update when I see the MRI and have more information. I just wanted to share the awesome news as soon as possible!

"The Lord is my light and my salvation; whom shall I fear? The LORD is the defense of my life; whom shall I dread? Though a host encamps against me, my heart will not fear; though war arises against me, in spite of this I shall be confident." (Psalm 27:1-3).

We have been at war with the enemy and God has prevailed! AMEN!

Carepage Entry: March 6, 2008 5:36 p.m.

I just saw the MRI comparison from 2/11/08 and 3/5/08 and I am overcome with emotion and gratitude. Praise the Lord for He has heard our prayers! *"He performs wonders that cannot be fathomed miracles that cannot be counted." (Job 5:9).*

Meredith's two MRI's were described as "dramatically different" by her oncologist. The difference, he said, was like "night and day." Her pediatric neurosurgeon came by and gave me a high five! He said the progress was "tremendous!" The tumors in her brain are still there, but the thickness and distribution is much thinner. Her spine looks even better as the tumors there shrank from 13.06 mm to 8.69 mm.

A couple of weeks ago, we were facing the loss of our baby, and today we stand before you in victory. No, these tumors are not gone, but they will be! We give all the glory to God. He has guided the hands of Mer's surgeons, her oncology team and her nurses, and we are claiming victory. When I thanked her oncologist, he said, "Don't thank me now. Thank me in two years." We don't think we will have to wait two years to thank him. We believe in miracles. We serve an awesome God who is in control of our daily decisions, who conducts miracles in the most dark and dreary situations.

We are still in need of intensive prayer. Meredith will start her second cycle of chemo on Monday, and I am sure we'll encounter other issues. But it is incredible to know and see that God is truly walking beside us through this whole thing. He gives us just enough—and sometimes a ton—of what we need to make it through each day. We are weak and tired; God knew we needed this to continue to fight. When we are weak, He makes us strong. I was reminded of how God called Moses to be a great leader. He had many excuses why God should not use him, but God revealed his perfect plan and, as we all know, used him for great and mighty things.

Thank you for all your prayers.

"This is the confidence we have in approaching God: that if we ask anything according to his will, he hears us. And if we know that he hears us—whatever we ask—we know that we have what we asked of him." (1 John 5:14-15).

When I received the call regarding Meredith's MRI, I cried with relief. All of the prayers, fasting and believing was working. I felt sure God was taking this disease in a different direction. Meredith's quick progress was indeed a miracle, but within weeks it seemed like our prayers did not work anymore. I could not grasp how it was God's will to take Meredith. I knew I was in His will and I was confident He was listening, so naturally I believed God would give me what I was asking for. It's not like I was asking for a new car. I was asking to spare the life of my child; a child who filled my life with insurmountable joy. A baby who could have given God the glory by following Him and changing lives for the Kingdom. She was just a baby.

For the first time, I, along with my friends and family,

could see a full recovery for Meredith. We believed Meredith would live. The surgeries and chemotherapy were successes in our minds. We were on the right path and I was so thankful. I felt strong in the Lord, but Satan used this time to mock my confidence in the Lord by whispering in my ear, "Beth, you are a fool to think God is going to cure her. You should know God is a fake." But the Holy Spirit was always close: "Beth, I brought Meredith back to you so you could make more memories, so she could meet her brother, so you could hear her say, "Ma, Ma" again. My plan was to heal her fully and to give her My best in Heaven. I knew she would only be on this earth for a short time when I created her, and I knew you needed more time with her before her real healing took place. You can trust me, Beth. Have I ever been unfaithful? Have I ever forsaken you? Remember who I am, Beth."

Carepage Entry: March 10, 2008 3:02 p.m.

We are thankful for a somewhat peaceful weekend before Mer's second week of chemo. We've had a few ups and downs over the last few days, but we've had things to rejoice every day as well. Meredith had an a-ha moment yesterday when she remembered how to use her pacifier! I put it in her mouth and she went to town sucking on that thing. It was fun to watch. She has always been a paci girl. Nurses also took off Mer's oxygen tube and took out an IV in her ankle. She had a busy day yesterday.

Today we were supposed to start chemo but her oncologist wanted to watch her temperature and get her nutrition level up through her feeding tube. So Meredith got another day of rest. There was also discussion about stepping up her medication to a more potent drug, but the doctor decided to stick with the last series of drugs. She responded well to the combination used last cycle. I was glad to hear this because I have been very apprehensive about starting a new drug this week. I just have had an uneasy feeling about it. God worked that out!

Meredith will start chemo tomorrow, so continue to pray for strength, protection and safety over her the next few weeks. We really don't know what to expect because Meredith was so sick before her first treatment. This time it will be very different. Also, I am tired. Because the hospital shut down visitation due to the flu, only parents of patients are permitted to be here all the time. I am amazed at how tired one can get just sitting in a hospital room hour after hour. The days and nights are endless.

In Philippians 4:6, God's Word says, "Do not be anxious about anything, but in everything, by prayer and petition, with thanksgiving, present your requests to God." This is so encouraging, but I have to admit that I am scared! I am looking at my baby who appears close to normal, and here we go again. Another frightening time awaits us. I am in a state of disbelief. "How can my baby have cancer?" "Is this really happening?" It is truly unbelievable and incomprehensible. But I know Meredith is going to get through this and she is going to do amazing things in her lifetime. I know God has a mighty purpose for her life. She has already changed so many lives and she has taught each of us so many lessons through this time of great stress. Today I was reminded that God picked me to be her mom and, no matter how hard this has been, she is a gift from Him. I wouldn't trade this baby, this moment in time, for anything else.

Meredith came back to us when the chemotherapy started to work. Miraculously, she acted more like herself every day. The moment she started sucking her pacifier again was the beginning of a priceless time when God gave her back to me. My family and friends firmly believed a miracle was going to take place. She was such a fighter. It looked promising. I am glad I savored every moment. I watched her like a hawk and I am thankful I was there. There were days I wanted to run away, but my love for her kept me strong. I am so thankful God gave me that time with her. We continued our usual patterns: I held her (just like I did at home), we watched TLC's *What Not to Wear* while we ate lunch, (just like we did at home) and we enjoyed being together (just like we did at home). There was no other place I wanted to be but by my girl's side. I needed her just as much as she needed me.

It became imperative during this time that Hunt and I work together, but that wasn't easy because we had two totally different ideas of what Meredith's care should entail. When Meredith was moved from PICU to the oncology unit, she did not have the continual presence of a nurse. It was up to Hunt and me to be there all the time. I never wanted Meredith to be alone. When she was awake, I wanted her to know her family was there to love on her. Hunt agreed to some extent but was not able to meet those expectations. I took the day shift so he could return to work, and he took the night shift. Since our families could not cover the time in between, due to a hospital "lock down," there were gaps when Meredith was left by herself. It was never for very long, but I still hated it. Some nights, Hunt was unable to come at all, and I was forced to choose between staying with Tyler or Meredith. I was incredibly torn at times, leaving my son for so long. He could not come to the hospital, so I would spend days away from him and nights exhausted, trying to care for him.

Once again, I was amazed at what was going on around me. I was living in a dorm room with my mother and an infant. There were two single beds, a bassinet for Tyler and a cot for the rotating family member on baby duty. During the day, women from my prior and present churches, parents of former students I'd taught and ladies from the singles ministry took turns caring for Tyler. People brought me books, CDs, food, flowers, journals, clothes and baby essentials. At night, my prayer group took turns being with me. They tried to lighten things up and help me feel as normal as possible. My support system was sturdy. God was blessing me abundantly and my only need and want was a cured daughter.

Carepage Entry: March 12, 2008 10:40 a.m.
"Never be afraid to trust an unknown future to a known God." Corrie Ten Boom

Meredith started her second round of chemo last night around 10 p.m. She seems to be doing well so far. She definitely has some nausea, but is sleeping right now. She is having trouble keeping down nutrients and some of the oral medication. Please pray that she can tolerate it.

In my devotion last night, this quote from Corrie Ten Boom really encouraged me. In a time of so much uncertainty, it's easy to not trust God and to hold onto fear. It is a minute-by-minute battle for me. I wish I had a crystal ball to show me the future, but I don't. I have to trust in the Lord that He is in control and that He is GOOD. I know that when I am at my weakest, that God is strong for me. That is my only explanation when people ask me how I'm making it through this. Each day God gives me the strength to come back to the hospital, to look at my daughter hooked up to tubes, to have hope that she will make a full recovery. There is no one else and nothing else in this world that can help me. God is my hope, my strength, my great defender. He has Meredith in His hands every moment of every day.

Please pray for strength, peace and comfort throughout this week. We need all the prayers we can get!

Although this was a tough day for Meredith, it was a glorious one for my mother. She received the best birthday present, being let back into the hospital to help care for Meredith. After being such a pivotal caregiver for so long, she was forced to leave Meredith two weeks earlier due to the shut-down. It nearly killed her. On my mother's 62nd birthday, through a miraculous connection, she was given the okay to come back by a hospital administrator. This was a huge relief to me. I was completely exhausted and alone. We had been a team up until the closing, and I was used to her being there to encourage and support me. After two weeks of being alone all day with Meredith, meeting with doctors on my own and making hard decisions on my own, I was elated my mother could join me again. I was worn out and the timing was perfect. Mom spent the night with Meredith and held her as she vomited from the chemo. She stood in my place when I wasn't strong enough to face it. Giving chemo to Meredith made me so conflicted, and I needed a reprieve desperately. My mother was unbelievably strong for a woman who was watching her daughter and granddaughter suffer.

Mom and I held Meredith as much as possible. We were encouraged by the staff to do so. It was frightening sometimes—there were multiple monitors, a feeding tube, arm and leg braces to avoid atrophy, and scars from surgeries. The thought of causing Meredith more pain by accidentally pulling on these lines was quite intimidating. But holding her close was critical. She needed to feel our love and we needed to hold her close.

I remember being very guarded and numb at this time. Even though the MRI had come back with positive results, I was still very scared. I certainly hoped that God would provide a full recovery. I held onto that, but deep down I knew that the statistics and research were against us. For a child with a non-disseminated case, aggressive surgery, radiotherapy and chemotherapy, the survival rate is 50 percent after five years. Roughly 80 to 90 percent of those without disseminated disease can be cured, but most survivors have lifelong neurologic and cognitive deficits. The survival rate was not as good for Meredith because of her age and the massive dissemination of cancer cells. The cancer had coated her central nervous system like icing on a cake, and she was too young to receive radiation. She was part of a high-risk group of children whose survival rate was only 30 to 35 percent over a five-year period. I was cautiously optimistic about Meredith's progress but God had not confirmed in my heart He was going to give her back to me. I knew it would be clear to me when He was ready to reveal Meredith's fate.

Carepage Entry: March 14, 2008 3:24 p.m.

We continue to be encouraged by what we have seen take place with Meredith. She made it through her three days of chemo with a lot of nausea and sickness, but that was to be expected. The next few days will be very challenging as we watch and wait to see progress. The doctors seem pleased with the positive changes over the last few weeks, and we have been delighted as well. That's what makes this cycle so difficult. Every day I see glimpses of my old Meredith and it makes my heart jump for joy. The thought of her getting chemo that makes her sick is hard to swallow. I know it has to be done, but it seems like torture. I have to remind myself where we've come from, though. A few weeks ago, we were discussing the logistics of her return home to Jesus, and here we sit looking at a child who seems like she could have a full recovery. I'm almost scared to say that because the future is so unclear. However, I feel a strong sense of peace right now from the Lord that, although it will not be a short road, it will be one that ends in a miracle.

Two days ago, I was talking to Meredith and I saw a smile. It was only a split second, but how sweet it was. I thought I might be dreaming or made it up, so I told only a few people. But today she smiled again, even after having three days of chemo! There is something so special about a child's smile. It's even more special when you haven't seen that smile is two months! What an amazing moment God gave me. Thank you, Lord!

I have been listening to a CD someone gave me, and I've been captivated by the lyrics in one song especially: "And how could I ever doubt You after all You have pulled me through?" We have been through every emotion over the past few weeks. Shock, despair, joy, grief, disbelief and doubt. But each day God gives us hope and, as I talk with others who have been through a similar journey, the same point is reiterated: "God will pull you through. Just trust Him and give Him all your worries and fears." It is easy to say this but so difficult to believe at times.

It was truly a miracle that I witnessed her smile again. Meredith was so strong and brave. After all she had been through; she mustered up a beautiful smile. In that dark and depressing room, my heart was full and God's presence was strong.

When Meredith was well, the joyful times were abundant. I would try to take a morning shower while she was in her crib, and it never worked. I could see her from my bathroom and she refused to play. She only screamed. She would cruise in her crib to the corner and wait for me to get her. She was a determined little one. I would beg her for a few more minutes, but she would not relent, so I'd rush to get ready and take her in my arms. It never made me angry—just happy that I could calm her and bring back that smile back to her porcelain face. I hoped and prayed that we would make more memories like these.

Carepage Entry: March 16, 2008 3:26 p.m.

Each day we are given so many gifts from the Lord. First of all, He has brought Meredith through so much in a short time. As I reflect on the past two months, everything seems like a big blurry nightmare. I cannot believe that a few weeks ago her tumors were putting so much pressure on her brain that she was in a coma. I was facing the loss of my first child. It is still hard to comprehend all that has happened. Although our journey is far from being over, I am encouraged each day by Meredith's progress. This week and weekend have been very difficult. Mer has felt terrible. Every time she is awake, she is crying. She has had so much discomfort and, as a mother, I have suffered with her. I truly feel her pain and would do anything to take it from her. I have to remind myself that she will not remember this time of her life. We will all remember but thank you Lord that she will not. What a comfort.

Yesterday, in the midst of all her pain, she gave me another gift. Meredith said "Ma, Ma" and she smiled several times in a row. Luckily, the nurse was in the room when Mer said it; otherwise I would have not believed it. I almost fell to the floor. I honestly didn't think I would hear those words for a long time. I guess I shouldn't have doubted her determination. She is such an amazing baby! It is hard to truly rejoice in times like this. As soon as the good moments pass, the fear returns. I have to keep reminding myself to praise God for how far we have come and to continue to have hope for the future.

I know I would not have made it this far without God's comfort and faithfulness. Even though my heart feels like it is broken into a hundred pieces, somehow He mends the pieces together by His mighty hands. Each time I feel lonely, stressed and depressed He brings me back with His promises. He has never left my side. Only He understands the pain I have endured. After all, He watched His son die on the cross for our sins.

Thank you for all your prayers. Never underestimate the power of them!

Merriam-Webster (2009) defines hope as "desire with expectation of obtainment." I wanted to have this kind of hope. I desired to be that person who expected a miracle with such vigor and might that I would receive it. However, my mind and heart processed the statistics of Meredith's particular circumstances, and I knew it was up to God to perform a miracle. I could not put aside my concerns and the frightening facts that doctors were communicating to me on a daily basis. Through the highs and lows I focused on Psalm 130:5, where David says, "I wait for LORD, my soul waits, and in his word I put my hope." I had to wait and see what God was going to do. My desires to fix this problem with solutions of my own accord never proved successful. God was carrying me through. It was when I was at the end of myself that He took over. Even though God and I differed dramatically on the fate of my baby girl, I continued then to hope in Him and still do today. "Be strong and take heart, all you who hope in the LORD." (Psalm 31:24).

Carepage Entry: March 19, 2008 2:31 p.m.

I cannot believe how fast our little Meredith has come back to life. There are no words to describe the drastic change that has taken place over the past few days. First of all, she has a lot more movement in her legs. They are pulling back when we tickle her feet or change her diaper. Secondly, her left arm is working really well. Her gross motor skills are coming back slowly but surely. She started rubbing her eyes yesterday as well as her nose (where her feeding tube resides). Unfortunately, last night she actually pulled out her feeding tube. That's our Meredith. When she doesn't like something she refuses to tolerate it! In another wonderful development, I was able to hold Meredith upright on my shoulder and she tolerated it quite well. Her neck is still very weak and will need to be strengthened with the help of physical therapy, but I was excited to see that she was not totally uncomfortable in that position. It was also a very special time for me to hold her close without fighting all the tubes and cords. I felt like our hearts were melting into each other. We all miss holding Meredith close and are excited each day we get closer to doing the things that we loved.

All of your prayers have touched our lives. We see God's hand in everything that has occurred. We've all come a long way in the last two months. Our lives will never be the same. But it seems that they needed some changing anyway.

Our journey is far from over. Meredith will rest for another week and a half, and then we begin chemo again. This time it will be 21 days of an oral drug. So we still need as many prayers as we can get. Her oncologist came in today and said, "She looks good!" He looked at her 9-month picture hanging in the room and said his goal was to get her looking like that again. We cannot wait.

By the way, Tyler is doing great. His actual due date was yesterday. He is starting to wake up more, which means our nights are sleepless. He is being loved like crazy by all of you who've come to watch him during the day. He is officially spoiled, which means both my arms will be holding a baby when Meredith comes home. I better start exercising those biceps.

I am going to add some pictures of Meredith in her new hospital gown. A dear friend heard that Mer was wearing a Duke-blue hospital gown and quickly made her a pink and white one. Meredith only does pastel colors.

As you are praying, please lift these up for Meredith:

Her white blood cell counts will be at their lowest on Sunday. Pray for protection from fever or illness. She is having slight seizures. Pray for these to be taken away completely. Pray for her to regain strength in her neck, arms, legs and back each and every day.

We love you and thank you for every prayer.

We are told to believe, pray, fast and pray some more. For some, it really works and their prayers are answered. For me, I do believe my prayers were granted and a miracle was performed, but not in the way I'd envisioned.

My Prayer: Lord, I need your guidance and strength. Tell me what I need to know and make me who I need to be! Sometimes, I feel You aligning my mind with Yours. But I still cannot find an answer to my question, "Why Meredith?" I cannot grasp why chemotherapy and surgeries work for some people but not others. On this earth, I will never know why my daughter was not healed and given back to me. But what I do know is that You are close to the brokenhearted and the crushed in spirit. (Psalm 34:18).

8

Home

Carepage Entry: March 22, 2008 8:59 p.m.

Meredith is out of the hospital! Yesterday, we were discharged from Duke at 3:30 p.m. There was talk earlier in the week about sending her home, which sent us all into a panic. It was good news but anxiety-provoking at the same time. Friday morning the oncologist came in and said, "Meredith looks great and you have all been in the hospital way too long. She needs to get some sunshine." So, we quickly got into action! There was so much to do. I had to get trained to use medical equipment and give 10 medicines, including an oral chemo medicine. How overwhelming! I kept asking God, "Why didn't you prompt me to go to nursing school versus being a teacher?" What a job for someone who hates math, especially the metric system!

Putting all those details aside, we are glad to have

Meredith home. It feels great to be out of the Ronald McDonald House, too. It certainly met the need, but there is nothing like being in a house with your own things and with people to help you. The first night on our own, Meredith was challenging. I've decided that I won't sleep again for the rest of my existence. All of Meredith's meds are on a 24-hour schedule. They are a full-time job! Mer's white blood cell counts are very low too. She is in isolation from most everyone right now. We will go back to Duke Monday for her first clinic visit. Hopefully, her counts will be on the way up. Please pray for Mer to steer clear from any infection. A lot of kids on chemo end up coming right back to the hospital due to fever once they are discharged.

As we celebrate Easter this year we have so much to be thankful for. First and foremost, we are grateful that our Savior was raised from the dead. Secondly, we are blessed to have made it through a very difficult and frightening time with Meredith. Lastly, we are thankful for Tyler's safe and easy arrival. Have a happy Easter Sunday!

I have had ups and downs that would put most people in the ground. This was a time in my life when intense joy and excitement coupled with monumental fear and distress. I was petrified when the doctor told us Meredith could go home. I questioned my ability to care for her round the clock. There was no way I could possibly tend to a cancer patient. On top of that, I came to the realization that I had no home! Hunt had locked me out and, frankly, I was afraid to go back to our old home after all that happened. At Duke and the Ronald McDonald House, I felt safe from Hunt as we had people all around us and there were rules and guidelines to follow. If we went back home, I would again be under Hunt's rules and intimidation. In my mind, it was simply not an option.

On the day of Meredith's release, Hunt demanded that I bring Meredith back to our marital residence—with restrictions on who could visit and when. He would keep my family away when he was there, requiring me to take care of two babies with his help only. But Hunt hadn't been present for the chemotherapy training or for all the meetings with Meredith's oncologist. I knew I couldn't do this without my mother and my support system, and I would not feel safe. I went into "fix-it" mode. I enlisted the help of my best friend Catherine and my father, and together we began to look at the possibilities—a furnished apartment, a larger room at the Ronald McDonald House, a friend's spare room. But nothing sounded appropriate. We needed space and protection, a place that was quiet, safe and nurturing. I called my sister and brother-in-law and said, "I need to bring my sick baby, my brand-new baby and myself to your house. We need to live with you."

Before Hunt, Kim and Mike had been my best friends. They cared for me. I would stay at their house when I was sick, scared or stranded without power during a storm. Mike didn't hesitate when I asked for help: "Come, we will make it work." God clearly knew what he was doing when he urged Mike and Kim to pick up their lives and relocate to North Carolina from Virginia 10 years earlier. He knew I would need them to take care of me as well as my children.

Carepage Entry: March 24, 2008 6:38 p.m.

As I stare at Meredith I am overcome with gratitude for her progress and strength. It has not been an easy adjustment being out of the hospital but I rejoice in the fact that we are in a warm, safe environment free from constant beeps, wires and hospital staff visits. Meredith, Tyler and I are staying with my sister and brother-in-law in North Raleigh. We are surrounded by family members who have been helping with Mer's 24-hour care. It has been a huge blessing to be here. I feel that angels are surrounding this house, watching over each of us and keeping us strong. The kids and I are lucky to have such a strong support system. We are also right off of I-540 so we can be at Duke in 25 minutes.

Today, Meredith had her first clinic visit at Duke's Children's Hospital. We were excited to learn that her counts are great! Her white blood cell count went from 800 (Friday) to 31,000 (today). God continues to remind us that He is in control. He has brought us so far. I was listening to a song on Sunday that asked, "If everything was taken away, would you still believe?" We've all had to ask ourselves this question. Would I still believe that God was good if He took my daughter? Would my faith still be strong? Would I celebrate Him and find joy in the most difficult situation? At times it feels that so much has been taken away. Our lives will never be the same, but God knew that and He will make things better than they ever were before. Thank you, Lord, for hope even in the midst of great darkness.

This past weekend had many wonderful moments, but it was full of battles and challenges. On Saturday night I asked the Lord to just give me a word directly. I felt exhausted, overwhelmed and totally unqualified to administer medications to a 1-year-old through a feeding tube. God gave me Psalm 70:1, 5: "Hasten, O God, to save me; O Lord, come quickly to help me...You are my help and my deliverer; O Lord, do not delay." I was at the end of my strength and resources and it was wonderful to *receive from His unlimited supply.*

Your prayers have and continue to make a difference in our lives. Thank you.

Moving into my sister's house was a relief, but it was also a frightening experience. I knew there would be tension between the families when I resisted returning home to Hunt. I had to repeatedly ask myself, "Am I doing this because it is right or because I am fearful?" I used to live in fear and made all decisions based on this emotion. But this was different. I couldn't be scared. I had to make a decision that would provide the safest and most supportive environment for my ill child and premature infant.

God's resources went right to work preparing her home for our arrival. Staff members from my brother-in-law's school came over and brought a crib, changing table and supplies. The neighborhood created a meal schedule and had food ready for us. My former place of employment collected paper goods, and my college friend brought snacks, household items and clothes. Our every need was being met. Mike and Kim's dining and living room were transformed into a hospital room complete with a single bed for me, a crib for Meredith and a medicine station. I walked in with a sigh of relief. It was also in this moment that my eyes, mind and heart were opened up to the abusive behaviors that had ruled me for so many years. As I settled in, Hunt threatened to charge me with kidnapping and to take Tyler away from me. Fear took hold, but my dear and faithful friends fell on the floor and prayed for our protection and peace. Once again God protected my babies and me, and Hunt never acted on his threats. He decided he would not see his children in my sister's home, and he upheld his promise without seeing Meredith the entire time she was out of the hospital. Finally, there was peace.

My Prayer: Lord, help me to always make my decisions based on what is right and not fear of consequences. Help me to never allow fear to consume me and to call upon Your name when I am paralyzed by my circumstances. I will always hold true to Your Word and fear only You, trust in only You—as You are my help and my shield in times of trouble. (Psalm 115:11).

9

Savor Every Moment

Carepage Entry: March 26, 2008 11:36 p.m.

After several sleepless nights we finally figured out what is plaguing little Meredith. Teeth! It is hard to believe that something normal is happening to her. She is getting two new top teeth. We had asked ourselves every question. Is it the chemo? Is she stiff? Is she sleepy? What is going on? We didn't even think about her getting more teeth. Even though she is miserable, we were happy to see her body doing normal things.

Every day is filled with exciting new developments with Meredith. God is restoring her day by day. Tonight as I put her to bed I just wept. Thank you God for giving me my daughter back. Thank you Lord for your mercy, your faithfulness, your promises of being good and true. Words cannot describe my gratitude for what the Lord has done.

Right now, Mer is pointing again, laughing (when she is

in a good mood, not on demand). Her right arm is starting to move a little bit, and she is putting her hands together. She also put her paci in her mouth. Every day is another miracle! We have a ways to go with her fine motor skills but, at this rate, she should be back to her old self in no time.

I know that I thank you every time I write, but the amount of support and love we have received is simply remarkable. I feel so unworthy of all you do for my family. Each of you has played such a pivotal role in this journey. I look forward to seeing God's plan revealed over the next few days, months and years. One thing is for sure, it is going to be glorious!

These moments meant so much to all of us. So many amazing events occurred in a small window of time. God gave us time to make more memories. Meredith was able to not only meet her baby brother but also to spend some time with him. We propped them up on the couch together and took tons of pictures. She looked at him like, "who is he?" I was so grateful to have them together. Meredith and I visited with family members who'd come from far away to support us. It was refreshing to be away from the hospital, but taking care of two babies was a test of my strength and confidence.

As Meredith became stronger, I was eager to hold her more. She was still hooked up to a pulse oximeter which monitored the oxygen saturation of her blood and a feeding tube, and maneuvering around them was challenging. But, holding her close and repositioning her was important to me. Some nights, I would put her in bed with me and just hold her in my arms all night long. When she was well, she always slept with me. She would start out in her crib, but in the middle of the night, she would cry and I was too exhausted to try to rock her back to sleep. Thus, she always ended up cuddled in my arms. It felt good to be able to do this again. There were many nights when I begged and wept before God as I held her tight. This was too hard. I was too weak. I wanted her to get better. I needed to know from God that He was going to heal her. I remained hopeful but mindful of the possibility of her not being healed on this earth. Every minute of every day I had to trust that the God who I had given my child to would hear my prayers and give me the miracle I was so desperately praying for.

Carepage Entry: April 1, 2008 6:08 p.m.

Being at home has been wonderful and totally overwhelming. All the family and friend support has been absolutely amazing. Our family has been so blessed by you. We want for nothing—our focus can be on Meredith and Tyler. Thank you for your prayers, cooking, cleaning, organizing, washing clothes, etc. God continues to remind me that without the body of Christ we would be in a constant state of confusion and chaos.

Yesterday, my Mom and I spent the entire day at the hospital. Meredith pulled out her feeding tube Sunday night. It was a bittersweet event. The good part is she wanted to get that thing out of her nose and she was able to maneuver her hand in a way to get it out. The bad part is we had to go to radiology and get it put back in. Try explaining to a 1-year-old the consequences of her actions (hee, hee). Meredith continues to do amazing things each day. She is making strides in every way. Her arms and legs are moving more. Her neck is getting stronger and she is regaining control of her back muscles. We thank God for her progress. Even though Mer continues to get better, there are times we grieve over where we have been and how far we have to go. I try not to focus on all the scars and the large shunt that protrudes from her head. My brain knows that without these imperfections Meredith would have died. But to see a baby who was once perfect with so many war wounds is sometimes more than I can take. I am reminded, though, that Christ's scars represented His sacrifice and His gift to us of washing away our sins. Maybe Mer's scars will be evidence to all of us how faithful and true God is and how much He has changed our lives through granting us this miracle.

"All things were made by him; and without him was not anything made that was made."(John 1:3). I am constantly amazed by my devotions. God gives me just what I need each time I need to be filled up. The title of this devotion is "Made and Repaired by The Master" by Corrie Ten Boom. She tells the story of a man who needs a place to stay. A family has a basement with a broken harp in it that could not be repaired. The man ends up fixing the harp to the owner's dismay. When he is asked how it was fixed, he replies, "I made this harp years ago, and when you make something, you can also repair it."(Ten Boom, 2000). How encouraging that every sign of Mer's illness can be repaired with God's tender touch.

Please continue to pray for Mer as she started her journey of 21 days of chemo. She feels rotten but, as usual, is fighting through each moment of each day.

Meredith was making progress at home. Some of her feistiness was coming out. She was slowly coming back to us, every day fighting for one more day. But we still had quite a battle ahead. Our days were spent giving Meredith Neupogen, Accutane, cleaning up vomit, changing her diaper, cleaning up vomit, giving her Zofran, cleaning up vomit, diaper, Benadryl, Reglan, vomit, diaper, vomit, Zofran, Etoposide, vomit, vomit, vomit and so on. Mom and I switched off every other night caring for Meredith. It was a family affair taking care of two babies who needed around-the-clock care. Dad, Joyce Lynne, Kim and Mike had Tyler duty. Somehow we made it through the days and nights filled with baby cries and machine beeps. I administered chemotherapy every night and forced medicines into Meredith's body. I remember feeling sick to my stomach as I gave her Etoposide each night. But I didn't have time to deal with my feelings. I would do anything to save her and, if that meant giving her a chemotherapy drug that would kill her cancer cells and make her sick, I would do it. These are the things you do for the people you love.

I spent a lot of time pondering God's goodness throughout this ordeal. I have no real answers to my pain. But I heard a sermon that encouraged me to not question God's character. I know I have many times. It's hard not to want to know, *why*? It's difficult to hear silence when you want answers. It's easy to blame Him for not giving me what I want. But, God promises to take care of His people, and when I accepted Him as my Lord and Savior, I put my trust in Him. It was time to walk in faith "by being sure of what [I] hope for and certain of what [I] do not see." (Hebrews 11:1).

My Prayer: I could not have made it through this time without You by my side. Thank you for being my everything. You're all I want in Heaven! You're all I want on earth! Whether I am at my weakest or my strongest, God is rock-firm and faithful. Thank you for doing what I could not do myself. Even though there is no end in sight to my pain, I feel the very presence of God—oh, how refreshing it is! (Psalm 73:25-26, 28, *The Message*).

10
Surrender

This week has been one of great joy and great challenges. Friday, we took Meredith to her physical therapy appointment to get an assessment. We were all very impressed with her muscle tone and progress. Watching her respond to the therapist and putting her in different positions was refreshing. Also, we were given a ton of new exercises to try with her and some very important information on her sensory integration issues. I was deeply encouraged by the PT's comments. She believed that a lot of Meredith's movements were voluntary. She also said that any movement is considered good. Mer seems to definitely be ahead of the gang for babies who experience brain trauma. So Friday was a good day!

But good days can turn bad in the blink of an eye. Saturday and Sunday Meredith threw up so many times.

I was very concerned and, as I held her Saturday night, I thought to myself, we cannot do this anymore. None of us can. It is too hard. I'm done and Mer is, too. We want this to be over with!

Last night, I was changing Mer and she had just thrown up a considerable amount. All of a sudden, she became unresponsive, similar to when she was in step-down several weeks back. It was a scary experience, and I was alarmed that her sodium levels went down again. So, we were off to Duke to get her checked out. After a five-hour visit, X-rays, a CT scan and blood work, Meredith got a good report. Thank you Lord, we did not have to stay overnight. Sometimes I look at these situations and I simply cannot believe this is all real. As I watched Mer get bundled up and put into a CT scan, it seemed like a bad dream. I still feel like this is an out-of-body experience. Am I really standing here watching her get her fifth CT Scan? Why my baby? How much more can we endure? Ugh, every action and thought is full of great stress and emotional energy. It is exhausting.

Today, as I listened to a sermon about missionaries Jim and Elisabeth Elliot, I was touched by their story. The Elliot's went to Ecuador in the 1950s to reach an Indian tribe that had never heard of Christ. Jim ended up a martyr, but his mission to reach the Auca Indians was taken over by his wife. God immediately impressed on my heart the importance of finding joy and being courageous in the midst of great challenges. I thought of my experience last night at the CT scan. Instead of seeing this as something traumatic, I need to find the joy in every situation. Instead of feeling overwhelmed and sad about Meredith and the other things we've encountered in the past two and half months, my goal will be to focus on the good. What a blessing it is that *doctors can scan my child's brain. What a gift it is that my baby was born in a time where chemotherapy has a high success rate. Thank you, Lord, for bringing my baby back from what looked like a horrible and senseless death. There are so many things to be thankful for. I pray I can achieve this goal in the coming minutes, days, months. I will need help and encouragement to stay positive, to rejoice in the little things, to wait on God's perfect timing, to be anxious about nothing.*

Please pray for Meredith, as she feels terrible. We are only on day six of our 21-day cycle of chemo. It is going to be a long month for all of us.

My family and I were in disbelief at how well Meredith's appointment went with the physical therapist. A short time ago, she couldn't move any limb. Now we were watching her lift her little head and respond to repositioning. My Aunt Joyce Lynne attended her PT appointment with me. We smiled and cheered at every sign of progress. I began to absorb every piece of advice from her PT. She showed me what kind of equipment Meredith would need, what exercises I needed to practice with her, and she gave me an idea of what we would need for the future. For the first time, we were talking about Meredith's future. It looked like things were only going to get better from here.

My skills as a "planner," a person "in charge" went to work. I knew I could handle it if Meredith needed special accommodations and equipment. I naturally organize, prioritize and strategize. I plan to avoid stress. I plan to avoid failure. I teach planning to people who have no plans. But how does a planner stop planning? I know the answer now—she stops planning when she faces a situation that cannot be controlled, not even a portion. God did not gently nudge me to stop planning. He demanded it. I was stripped of everything I depended on. All I had was Him. I surrendered my child, my marriage, my career, my security and safety to Him. God actually had to pry every piece out of my clutched fists. I had to let go of control. I pressed into the Lord for every decision. I lived one day at a time when it came to Meredith because, in the blink of an eye, it could all change.

My Prayer: Lord, teach me to surrender all to You. When I get the urge to devise a plan for my life, shut the doors that I keep trying to pry open. It is hard to remember Your plans are always righteous and good when our lives take paths so different than what we'd anticipated. Solidify Jeremiah 29:11 in my heart and mind: "For I know the plans I have for you," declares the Lord, "plans to prosper you and not to harm you, plans to give you hope and a future."Help me to place my faith in You and give thanks.

11

Finality

Carepage Entry: April 10, 2008 7:06 a.m.

POSTED BY CATHERINE

Beth asked me to send out a note asking you to join us in prayer regarding Mer's latest situation. She was taken to Duke last night because her breathing was labored and she was really struggling from throwing up so much.

The doctors did X-rays, CT scans and much more. They discovered that Meredith has the onset of pneumonia as well as a possible tear in her esophagus. She was admitted to the PICU for care, and we are thankful God gave Beth and her Mom the wisdom to go immediately to Duke. Yesterday Meredith's white blood counts were very low and that will mean she has to fight harder to rid her body of this infection. I know she is in good medical hands but, even more importantly, she is in God's hands. So many of you have shared that Meredith is a living miracle in our day. Please join me in continuing to see the miracle completed for our sweet, sweet Mer.

Please pray for:

1. The family to have the strength and peace to walk through this storm knowing God is in control.
2. The antibiotics to quickly attack the pneumonia and heal her from this sickness.
3. Supernatural rest in this difficult time. Beth has been up 10 days straight caring for Tyler and Meredith.
4. Protection from sickness for the family as they get physically run down from this journey.

New information:

Beth just found out that doctors have ordered an MRI on Meredith this afternoon. This is overwhelming for them because it will show the results of the chemo. I am asking you to claim God's healing over this MRI. I am begging the Lord to allow Meredith to have had miraculous results and that the cancer will have been destroyed. Thank you again for all of your care, support, prayers and encouragement. I will let you know the results when I hear.

Our God is in control!

I had so much hope, but Meredith kept getting worse. I prayed so much my knees were bruised. It was so hard to accept that this was happening to my family. How did we get this hand of cards? When Mom and I took Meredith back to the hospital the second time, she became unresponsive and showed signs of abnormal posturing (an involuntary flexion or extension of the arms and legs, indicating severe brain injury). It had gotten significantly better with treatment but returned with a vengeance this night. In the PICU the doctor ordered an anti-seizure drug, and I kept saying, "She's not having seizures. Her oncologist said she is not having seizures." The doctor just kept working and giving her more drugs to treat her symptoms. I remember looking at her with great conviction that I knew what was happening, but I really did not.

Mom and I sat there until the PICU doctor got Meredith stable at 2 a.m. I tried to keep it together so I could explain to the nurses what drugs she needed. She had to get everything on time. I was panicked that she had missed her chemotherapy dose. The doctor called Meredith's oncologist and confirmed that they could hold off on the chemotherapy. Getting the seizures under control was critical. Out of desperation, I was trying to control anything I could. I am sure the doctors knew the severity of the situation, but Mom and I could not even go there. The doctors and nurses strongly encouraged us to go home and get sleep. We resisted at first, but acquiesced with assurances that Meredith was stable. We left to sleep for a couple of hours. I don't know how I lived through that night. Perhaps it was denial, or the Holy Spirit, or just fatigue.

As I woke on April 11, my heart was heavy with grief. This was the end to our battle and I knew I was facing the most dreadful and difficult experience of my lifetime. I asked my best friend to update Meredith's Carepage as I didn't have the energy to write. I called the PICU to speak with Meredith's nurse. She informed me that Meredith was resting but was having some difficulty breathing. We needed to get there soon. My Mom and I arrived at 10 a.m. In the PICU waiting room, as I sat and waited to be buzzed into Mer's room, I observed a new family that sat with me. They had the same last name as ours. Their daughter, 14 years old, had suffered a brain aneurism that nearly killed her. She was approaching her death just like my daughter. This girl's mom asked me if I was okay, and I began to cry. We embraced. Our daughters were both going to die, and we knew it. It was then that God told me it wouldn't be very long till Meredith met Him in Heaven.

Carepage Entry: April 12, 2008 12:08 a.m.

POSTED BY CATHERINE

I know so many of you have been praying and joining us on our knees for Meredith and her family. I am writing tonight to share such difficult news. The MRI results show that Meredith's cancer has spread a great deal. Her doctor does not feel they can continue the chemo under the circumstances. The family is grieving this information, and we are all at a loss for words. I ask that you join me on my knees to our Savior.

As my family, best friend and I waited for the results of the MRI, we sat in silence. Finally, I got the call from Meredith's pediatric oncologist. In an anguished voice he said, "It's worse. The cancer has spread and there is no longer need for treatment. Beth, there is nothing else we can do." I fell to the floor screaming. I kicked and flung myself all around. The pain was intolerable. I wanted to die. My girl was dying. God was letting me baby die. Those who loved me held me tight, crying, begging God to comfort me.

On April 12, we had to begin discussing the logistics of Meredith's death. Did we want to stay at the hospital or go home with hospice? Was it going to be hours or days? What should we expect? I just lay beside Meredith crying as I made decisions on the final days of her life. I decided it would be best for Meredith to die in the hospital surrounded by her family. During this time, my friends and family came to comfort me. The pastor from a church I'd attended years before also visited. He had shared a similar experience with his youngest son a couple of years earlier. His child was at the same hospital with the same pediatric surgeon. I yearned to hear something from this pastor to ease my pain and suffering. As he stood beside me and stared at my child, I said, "She is my everything. I cannot live without her." He paused and said, "God never intended for a human to be our everything." Silently, I agreed. I knew that God was and had to be my all in all.

Meredith was being kept on a ventilator because her doctors knew there was a possibility she would die without it. Her pediatric oncologist informed us that she could stay on it for another day or two. But her heart rate was 230 and she was clearly in distress as the anesthesia from her MRI lifted. It became imperative that we remove the ventilator. I relayed the message to Hunt and, with some convincing, he gave his consent to remove it. He would not be present, though.

As the doctors and nurses prepared to remove the ventilator, I held my baby tightly with the knowledge that in minutes she could be dead. My mom and dad, sister and I watched and prayed as the nurse removed the tube. By God's grace, Meredith breathed on her own. I quickly scooped her into my arms and we were whisked away to the oncology unit for comfort care.

Emotions were running high when Hunt and his family returned to the hospital. We began to debate about who would be in the room with us for Meredith's final days. We could not agree and an argument broke out. I insisted that only family members be allowed to stay, but Hunt wanted friends there, too. In the heat of our discussion, a family member of Hunt's, who was previously very close to me, came into the room and announced publicly that Meredith's death was the result of a specific sin of my past. Hunt joined in with his agreement. My mother, Joyce Lynne and I gazed in disbelief. The events that followed included mediation with the hospital social worker, among other things. Until that moment, I'd never pondered Meredith's cancer being my fault. Honestly, I would never have connected these two tragedies.

My marriage was over at that very moment. I would never again trust and love someone who shouted my past sins and weaknesses to the world. That incident also made me revisit God's forgiveness and its meaning. I knew that God had paid for my sins on the cross and I was forgiven. Although exposure of my deepest, darkest secret caused me great distress and anxiety, it also freed me. "He who conceals his sins does not prosper, but whoever confesses and renounces them finds mercy." (Proverbs 28:13).

My Prayer: Lord, I thank you for your mercy and grace; for never using my sins against me, for forgiving my sins and loving me unconditionally. I understand that You do not waste pain. Open my eyes to the truth and help me surrender once again all that I am to You. Do as You wish with my life. You have complete control of it.

"All that I am—my assets…my strengths…my liabilities…my fears… anxieties…hurts…past sins…reputation—all of these I leave with Him." (Cheryl Biehl, 2000).

12

God Whispered "Fourteen"

Carepage Entry: April 14, 2008 1:35 p.m.

POSTED BY CATHERINE

I wanted to share the heartfelt news about our sweet, sweet Meredith Elisabeth Edwards. She passed away peacefully this morning at 7:15 a.m. in the arms of her family. We are thankful to know that she is in God's arms. She has been a witness to us all, and I know we will always cherish that. Please continue to pray for this family to be enveloped in the comfort and peace of our Lord and Savior throughout this difficult time. We will honor the celebration of Meredith's life with beautiful pink flowers for our sweet princess. Please join us in this celebration by wearing something pink in her honor.

On April 14, 2008, my 14-month-old Meredith Elisabeth died and went to Heaven. The number 14 has mixed meanings for me. It's the day that I dread each month, but it reminds me, too, that God speaks to me when I am willing to listen. God whispered in my ear, "fourteen" on April 12. I told Mom and Joyce Lynne what I had heard, but no one else. I didn't want people to think I was trying to be a prophet or that I was hearing voices. I'd never heard God's voice before, but there was no mistaking it. Meredith was 14 months old when she died on the 14th day of the month. It was an example of God's mercy and grace. When Mer's doctor and staff said it could be days or weeks, I just begged God to take her. Visions of cancer cells multiplying and destroying her were too much for me to bear. God knew I could not watch her die for days, weeks, months, so he gave me the number 14, and I waited in shock till that day arrived.

The days preparing for Meredith to die were painful—not for her, quiet and peaceful—but for me. I was so frightened to watch her die that I prayed to be asleep when it happened. I'm glad I wasn't. On April 13, my family went home, except for my mom and Joyce Lynne. They sat to my right as I held Meredith in the bed. Hunt and his family were on the other side of the room. My mom and aunt encouraged me to sleep. They would stay awake and keep track of Meredith's progress. Fortunately, Joyce Lynne was an oncology nurse and knew the stages of death. She knew the signs and would wake me if need be. Periodically, I would startle and ask, "Is she dead?" and they would tell me how her breathing had slowed. Two minutes before Meredith passed, she nudged me with her arm (though she hadn't moved in days) and I woke up. My mother and aunt had been counting her breaths, and they confirmed this had happened. I cuddled her into my arms and she soon took her last breath. I held my precious baby and gave her back to the One who gave her to me.

The hours after Meredith's death were hard to describe. Her surgeon and oncologist came by to hug us and share in our sorrow. Additionally, Meredith's main PICU nurses came and wept with us. I was given the option for the nurse to take Meredith and bathe her or do it myself. I chose to do it. Then I asked to take her to the morgue area where the hearse would get her. It was an unusual request but they allowed it. I wanted to spend as much time with Meredith as I could. Even though her spirit was gone, I needed to hold on to her as long as I could. I placed her into a baby casket and left. Our time at Duke was over. The day I dreaded was over. Meredith, a perfect gift sent from above, was gone.

"Sometimes we want things we were not meant to have. Because he loves us, the Father says no. Faith is willing not to have what God is not willing to give. Furthermore, faith does not insist upon an explanation. It is enough to know his promises to give what is good—he knows so much more about us than we do." (Elliot, 2000).

My Prayer: I am deeply grieved, disappointed and frustrated with Your choice to take Meredith. I firmly believe that You could have kept the cancer cells from ever appearing. I trusted You to annihilate the cancer as it was killing my child. I had faith in modern medicine and the physicians who worked tirelessly to save my child. I know You could have changed the course of events in an instant. I also realize that You said no. I will accept this and will live without demanding an explanation.

13

Meredith the Missionary

It is hard to put into words my thoughts and feelings about the last three months. As I reflect on Meredith's life, there is much joy and great sorrow. It would take days to recount all of the lovely moments I had with Meredith. She was truly a gift. It is still unbelievable to me that she is gone. My mind knows she is in Heaven, free of any pain and suffering, but my heart aches. It feels like it has been shattered into millions of pieces. But Meredith was only on loan to me from God.

I remember hearing before I had a child that as parents it is our responsibility to dedicate our children to the Lord. Many of us say we have given our kids to the Lord but place conditions on Him: "Lord, You can have her but just don't send her to Africa or far away." It is frightening to fully give our children to the Lord because then He can do anything with them. One of the recurring thoughts I've had since Meredith's death is that she was a missionary. I've always thought of missionaries as people who go to other countries to spread God's Word, but we are all called to be missionaries in our own community. Meredith's life was used for good. God's taking her will be used for good. We serve a good God.

After talking with doctors about Meredith's last MRI, we learned they were surprised she lived as long as she did. Although the MRI after her first treatment cycle was generally encouraging, it showed some tumors remaining that were resistant to chemotherapy. These cells multiplied fast and, in her final MRI, the tumors were so thick in her brain there was no way she could live no matter what chemotherapy was tried. At the end, Meredith's death was peaceful. I feel blessed that she died in my arms. I wouldn't have wanted it any other way.

God has given me many thoughts over the last three months. One was of Valerie Schnurr, who was in the library at Columbine High School on April 20, 1999. She was asked to denounce God while a gun was held to her head. She refused and Dylan Klebold reloaded his gun.

I've thought of Valerie's story many times. If someone was holding a gun to my head, would I still hold onto my faith? In a way I have faced this question. Meredith's diagnosis of cancer and her death have nearly taken my life and I'm asked to still believe. How could I not when Meredith was taken for a reason? As humans, we look at the length of our lives, but God looks at the impact of our lives. Meredith accomplished what she was put on this earth for. Can I be angry about that?

Tomorrow we will bury Meredith's beautiful body. It will be a day of great sadness, but I know that she will live in our hearts and one day I will see her again. I can envision her running to me as I enter into eternity.

I was in shock, despair and weakened, but felt strength and peace through Christ's Word and presence. I know with deep conviction that God has a plan for our lives and, way down the road; I might come to understand how losing my daughter to cancer had a purpose.

God used Meredith's illness and death, and I believe He will continue to do so. I am just holding on to His grace and strength to make it through each day. God has proven faithful as He is not only carrying me through my pain but catapulting me forward. The numbness continues, but I am alive. Honestly, I didn't know if I would make it a day without Meredith. I must rely on the Lord to get me out of bed each morning and to take each breath. My strength comes only from Him.

Carepage Entry: April 20, 2008 10:08 p.m.

The purpose of the Carepages has been to update you on Meredith, but I feel God pressing upon my heart to continue writing in Mer's honor. I will not be offended if you delete the e-mails or are just tired of hearing what I have to say. Writing is therapy for me. I find myself constantly reflecting on our journey over the last few months.

For those of you who could not attend Meredith's funeral, I want you to know it was absolutely beautiful. The Shutterbugs dress shop donated an amazing dress for her to wear. It was as long as her casket and was embroidered with pearls and ornate smocking. She wore a matching bonnet and looked perfect. Not a blemish showed, and it was a wonderful last image of her.

Although Meredith's funeral was one of the hardest

things I have endured, it was a time of great joy too. I was amazed at how many people had grown to love my little girl. The service included a slide show and I laughed and wept as I viewed it. Meredith brought so much joy to our lives but for me she has done so much more. In a way, she saved my life by changing it. I am thankful that God used her death to bring about His purposes in my life.

One comment made to me early in this journey has stayed with me. My Aunt Beverly said many times, "God is going to give you Meredith back 100 percent. I believe she will be totally healed." In the world's eyes, it looks like this didn't come true. But the only way Meredith would ever be perfect was if she was taken to Heaven. She is now 100 percent cancer free and she is full of joy, pointing at all the beauties of Heaven as the Father holds her. Meredith lives on with no disabilities, no obstacles, no conflict—just peace and comfort. At times it is hard to remember this. The grief can be unbearable. I cannot imagine anything hurting as much as this and I'd do anything to get my sweet baby back. But my family reminds me that, even though a place in my heart will always remain vacant, His love is sufficient. God will keep me going. He will give me more than enough of what is needed to keep me alive and hopeful. What an amazing God we serve.

Meredith looked like she was sleeping peacefully at her funeral. Most of all, she looked like herself. The beautifully beaded bonnet covered the shunt on the top of her head. The long white and pearl gown sheltered the incisions in her chest. What an exquisite sight. Seven hundred people attended her service. She was cherished by all who heard of her. God used Meredith in a mighty way.

My Prayer: Lord, there is nothing that anyone can do to

help me. You are the only One who can comfort me and give me a reason to go on. I must keep moving forward with Your help. I have to see this journey through so I can see what You can do with so much tragedy. I know in the end good will come of what I have endured. I'm holding on to Your promise in Psalm 119:50: "My comfort in my suffering is this: Your promise preserves my life." Please guide me and never let me be tempted to give up. I am so weak and I need Your strength to keep believing. Finish Your good work in and through me so that one day I can join with others in saying, "I have brought you glory on earth by completing the work you gave me to do." (John 17:4).

14

Trading Dreams

Carepage Entry: Posted Apr 25, 2008 6:10 p.m.

I have been so blessed by all of your cards and letters of encouragement and support. It warms my heart to know that Meredith touched so many of your lives in such a short time. She was such a special baby. I miss her so much. There is not one minute of each day that I don't think of her. It still seems like a bad dream, like I am living in a constant nightmare. To say that I am sad is a huge understatement. I am completely devastated, completely confused and totally conflicted. Grief is such a strange feeling. One moment I am trying to be "normal" by doing regular things, and the reality is I will never be normal again. I will never look at the details of life in the same way. I have to get used to a new normal, one that includes great sadness as well as immense hope.

I remember when I got pregnant with Tyler I just could

not believe it. Having a 1-year-old and a newborn was not exactly an ideal situation. I cried when I found out mainly because I thought I wouldn't have enough quality time with Meredith or with this new baby. Plus, the idea of getting up every three hours with a new baby was not at the top of my list. I remember questioning why I got pregnant so quickly after Meredith's birth. Now, as I look at my little boy sleeping, it is all so clear. God knew that I would not be able to survive this without Tyler. Every time I get really sad, he needs me. I get out of bed each day because I have him. He was God's gift, His way of keeping me on my toes, and a reason for me to feel some joy in the midst of so much sadness. I thank God for knowing just what I needed to get me through this tragedy.

Sometimes I cannot help but wonder why Meredith had to be the one to have cancer, and why she was not healed on this earth. I would do anything for it to be different. I would give anything to see her again, to touch her, to smell her. Why my baby? Why did my baby— who was my life, my identity, my best friend—get this rare cancer? It's so confusing, but many people keep reminding me to hold on to what I know about God. He is a good God. He will give me enough to get through each day and He will comfort me in this time of great despair.

In Philippians 3:14, the Bible says, "I press on toward the goal to win the prize which God has called me heavenward in Christ Jesus." It is my responsibility to use each day, each hour, each moment to be willingly inconvenienced and used for the Lord. Meredith has been a reminder to me that every day counts. None of us know what time we have left to serve, so all of our actions and words should leave a mark for the Lord.

The last three months were like being in a raging hurricane.

There were life-and-death decisions to be made, crises to be dealt with, drugs to be given and many sleepless nights. Now I am forced to pick up the pieces and go on. I feel like I am in the eye of the storm just waiting for the winds to pick up again. Last night I was totally surprised to see in my devotion this encouragement, "God will never leave you alone to face your problems. He guides you into the eye of the tornado where it is quiet and still, where you can hear His voice and feel the strength of His presence." (A Gentle Spirit, 2000). Oh, how I long to hear His voice. I have so many questions about His plan for my life. I know God wants the best for me but how can taking Meredith be the "best" for me? In my mind, the best would be having Meredith here, cancer free, laughing and playing, running around with her best friend Lily and her cousins, Parker and Jack. It just doesn't make sense.

I have asked this question of my God, friends and family, and the response is the same: God's ways are not our ways, and we see only the pieces of the puzzle rather than the whole thing. One day I hope to see the whole picture, but I have a feeling it will be when I am holding Meredith in my arms again.

Enduring a tragedy of this scale can drive you to the Lord or turn you away from Him forever. I am grateful I chose to wrestle with Him through the pain, sorrow and disappointment. I have spent a great deal of time asking God some tough questions and am eager to fill in the gaps between God's promises and God's provisions. There are times I want to give up. I feel like God failed me miserably. My precious daughter is dead, my marriage is over, I have a child who needs me and I have so little to give. Everything is a struggle. My soul aches with anger, guilt, despair, confusion and conflict. I wish God had given me an answer other than the one I received.

As I press into God with all my might, I know I cannot do this on my own. But He can. Romans 5:3-5 says, "rejoice in our sufferings, because we know that suffering produces perseverance; perseverance, character; and character, hope. And hope does not disappoint us, because God has poured out his love into our hearts by the Holy Spirit, whom he has given us." Thank you, Father, that You have brought God's love into my heart through the Holy Spirit. Thank you for giving me grace when I am angry and disappointed. When I come to You with my frustrations and questions You never fail me and always remind me You are in control of my life.

As children and even young adults, we have a dream for our lives. Mine was to be a wife and mother. When God made my dream come true and Meredith was born, I was so grateful. Then the very God who fulfilled my dream took it away. It feels unfair, unjust. Earth shattering. As I've begged God for clarity, my pleading has been met over and again with a question: "Would you trade your dreams for His?" Am I willing to trust God's plans for my life or am I going to trust my own? Certainly it would be easier to take my broken life and try to repair it with the things this world offers. But doing it my way would only be a temporary fix. My shattered life can only be repaired God.

It is true that few people on this side of Heaven endure so many tragedies at one time. They usually take place over the course of a lifetime. Not for me. I lost almost everything in the span of three months. I lost my marriage, my child, my money, house and security. The road to recovery is long and hard. It is a pilgrimage that God knew I would face. He knew I would watch my daughter thrive and develop into a lovely toddler, and He knew I would watch her suffer and die of brain cancer. He also knew I would survive her death even though I'd yearn some days to leave this world to be with her. There were so many good times with Meredith. She made me a better person; she made me want to be the best mom in the world. I never imagined I wouldn't have her to hold, to tickle, snuggle with and to pour all my love into. This is God's mystery that maybe in time He will reveal to me. For now, I continue to wrestle with God as Jacob did in Genesis 32:24-30, and I will not let go until God blesses me.

My Prayer: Lord, what dreams do you have for me? Show me as I travel on this lonely and challenging road. Help me to know you more intimately. Help me to know You are with me. All of my dreams, my hopes and goals have been shattered. Help me to find encouragement in the past—in the men and women who were destitute, persecuted and mistreated but who were commended for their faith in the end. (Hebrews 11:37-39). I have traded my dreams for Yours, Lord. I beg You to take them to greater heights than I could have ever imagined.

"So Jacob was left alone, and a man wrestled with him till daybreak. When the man saw that he could not overpower him, he touched the socket of Jacob's hip so that his hip was wrenched as he wrestled with the man. Then the man said, "Let me go, for it is daybreak."

But Jacob replied, "I will not let you go unless you bless me."

The man asked him, "What is your name?"

"Jacob," he answered.

Then the man said, "Your name will no longer be Jacob, but Israel because you have struggled with God and with humans and have overcome."

Jacob said, "Please tell me your name."

But he replied, "Why do you ask my name?" Then he blessed him there.

So Jacob called the place Peniel, saying, "It is because I saw God face to face, and yet my life was spared." (Genesis 32:24-30).

"For everyone who calls on the name of the Lord will be saved." (Romans 10:13).

Knowing Christ is the most thrilling and life changing decision you will ever make. God promises to give us strength in times of distress, comfort in our affliction (2 Corinthians 1:4) and deliver His followers to Heaven (John 6:38-40). If you do not know Christ as your personal Savior, take the time to say this prayer:

Dear God,
I believe You sent Your Son, Jesus, to die for my sins. I ask You now to forgive me for the things I have done wrong and be my Lord and Savior. Thank you for saving me, Lord!

Welcome to the family of faith!

Acknowledgments

First, to Christ: Thank you for giving me hope and a future, for giving my baby girl a new life of absolute bliss and joy in eternity, for blessing me with my beautiful son, Tyler, and an amazing support system.

To my family: Thank you for walking beside me so closely that I never felt alone and for giving me the strength to survive my greatest fears. Mom, you imparted such incredible wisdom and objectivity. You were the best birthing coach ever and you continue to be a woman I admire. Thank you for loving Meredith and standing in my place when I could not bear watching her pain. Dad, I cannot express my love for you in words. You always treat me like gold. I brag about you all the time because you have spoiled me with unconditional love, hugs and, of course, countless $20 bills for gas. Thank you for doing night duty with Tyler, even though he was always drenched after drinking his bottle. Kim and Mike, you are an amazing example of a loving couple and best friends. You have always been there for me. Thank you for taking in my family when we had nowhere to go, for allowing your home to be used as a family hotel, and for supporting us financially and emotionally after Meredith died. Your gifts have been truly sacrificial. Aunt Joyce Lynne, your contagious optimism, spirit, encouragement and wisdom are qualities I dream of possessing. You walked with me through Meredith's illness and you were a fortress around me when I was weak and vulnerable. Thank you for doing night duty with Tyler and for being by my side when Meredith left this earth to join Jesus. Mama 2, you are the most amazing grandmother. Thank you for praying for me since the day I was conceived. Your wisdom and knowledge of scripture has deepened my faith and my trust in the Lord. Aunt Bev, your prayers and encouragement were vital to my journey. Thank you for holding me accountable with this book by pushing me to get it done. Thank you also for holding my baby girl all night so she would feel the love and comfort of her family's arms instead of the coldness of her hospital bed. Finally, thank you for guiding me to do what was right and to stop living in fear.

To my friends: Cat, you are the absolute best friend in the world. You sacrificed so much for me. Thank you for talking countless hours on the phone with me, holding me accountable and listening to my pain. You were like a mother to Meredith and loved her like one of your own. I am grateful that you loved and supported me and you challenged me always with the question, "What is God telling you, Beth?" To my prayer group of six years (Cat, Catherine, Julie, Sybil, Anna Marie), your prayers, dedication and encouragement during the most horrific years of my life have been indescribable. You dropped to your knees without hesitation while I was in crisis and you came to the Ronald McDonald House weekly to help me feel "normal." I am forever grateful God gave us one another. Rene, I am blessed to call you my friend. You are the most sacrificial and humble woman I know. Thank you for your quiet yet powerful urge to serve others with no recognition or payment. You truly embrace God's call in <u>Colossians 3:12</u> to "clothe yourselves with compassion, kindness, humility, gentleness and patience." I admire your heart and yearn to give as you do. To my college suitemate, Jenny, your humor and strength during the last 11 years of my life have lifted my spirits and given me laughs when they seemed unattainable. Thank you for your care, concern and for reading my book in its original form and again right before publication. You are a trustworthy and faithful friend. Jackie, when your daughter came into my sixth grade class in 2003, I had no idea how precious you all would become to me. You are an amazing woman of God, and I cannot even begin to put into words what you did for me when Meredith was alive and well and when she was sick and dying. Thank you for organizing the supplies, buying Tyler a whole new wardrobe, taking care of Meredith in the hospital, collecting money and standing by my side in court. You are a true friend and confidant.

To my church families: Women of Faith Baptist Church, your prayers, love and encouragement during Meredith's short but meaningful life were crucial to our journey. Thank you for organizing meals, collecting money and visiting us in the hospital. To my Providence Baptist Church family, you came alongside me in the midst of such great despair. Your assistance logistically, spiritually and financially was pivotal to my recovery. Pastor Brian, thank you for your words of wisdom and for giving an amazing word from the Lord at Meredith's funeral. To the Bayleaf Baptist Joy Bible Study, your prayers, gifts and encouragement gave me the strength to get through each day at Duke. In addition, your beautiful and elegant sanctuary was the only place for Meredith's funeral. It was a gorgeous place to celebrate her life. Thank you for hosting a wonderful open house after Meredith's burial and treating me like part of your church family.

To my publishing team: Michele, you took my vision of this book cover and made it come alive. God has blessed you with a soft heart and creativity that can only be described as a God-given talent. Katie, I love you not only for your creative eye with photography but also for your tender heart and sacrificial spirit. You are an amazing photographer and a true friend. To Lundie's photography I treasure the CD you made of Meredith for me. Thank you for taking amazing pictures of her and letting me use them freely. Michelle, I was so blessed by your photo shoot of Tyler. You were incredibly generous to us and I will cherish the photos of him forever. Karen, I love you for reading my original manuscript and saying "no" to editing it. You are so wise! I appreciate your later help with my cover write-up. Jeannie, thank you for taking my first draft and making sense of it. You were so gentle with me as you made changes. Thank you for listening to God's voice while editing. You have been such a blessing to my life. I could not have done this without you.

To find out more about Beth Eastman, visit her blog, http://fourteenmeercies.blogspot.com/or email her at beth@tradingdreams.org

Edited by Jeannie Norris

Cover Design by Michele Castillo
(http://www.sonscapecommunications.com)

Author Photograph by Katie Mayer
(http://katiemayer.com)

Photographs of Meredith by Lundie's Photography
(http://lundiesphotography.com)

Photographs of Tyler by Michelle Prince
(http://www.michellestudios.com)

References

www.biblegateway.com

www.carepages.com/carepages/MEE2007

Biehl, Cheryl. (2000). Coming Before the Holy God of Heaven. *A Gentle Spirit.*

Casting Crowns. *Somewhere in the Middle.* (2007). Retrieved September 26, 2010, from elyrics: http://www.elyrics.net

Edward R. Rosick, D. M. (2010). *Medulloblastoma.* Retrieved August 26, 2010, from Answers.com: http//www.answers.com/topic/medulloblastoma

Elliot, E. (2000). Faith is Holding Out Your Hand. *A Gentle Spirit* .

Elliot, E. (1978). *The Journals of Jim Elliot.* Grand Rapids: Baker Book House Company.

hope. (2009). Retrieved July 3, 2009, from Merriam-Webster Online Dictionary: http://www.merriam-webster.com/dictionary/hope

Jones, R. (1999 , April 27). *Rocky Mountain News.* Retrieved April 20, 2008, from http://www. rockymountainnews.com

Moore, B. (2008). *Esther: It's Tough Being A Woman.* Nashville: LifeWay Press.

Roger J. Packer, M. C. (2009). *Medulloblastoma.* Retrieved July 3, 2009, from The Childhood Brain Tumor Foundation: http://www.childhoodbraintumor.org

"Swift Raging River", Unknown Author.

Ten Boom, Corrie. (2000). Made and Repaired by the Master. *A Gentle Spirit.*

Tobey MacDonald, M. (2009, February 12). *Medulloblastoma.* Retrieved August 26, 2010, from

EMedicine from WebMD: http://emedicine.medscape. com/article/987886-overview

Wells, C. (Composer). (2005). Held. [N. Grant, Performer] Raleigh, North Carolina, United States of America.

Unless otherwise indicated, all scripture quotations are taken from the New International Version (NIV)

9 781432 755515